T0340814

A SHORT
HISTORY
of the
WORLD *in*
50 PLACES

A SHORT HISTORY
of the
WORLD *in*

50 PLACES

Dr Jacob F. Field

Michael O'Mara Books Limited

This book is dedicated to Grandma Billie and Nana,
and in memory of Al and Aussie Granddad.

First published in Great Britain in 2020 by
Michael O'Mara Books Limited
9 Lion Yard
Tremadoc Road
London SW4 7NQ

A CIP catalogue record for this book is available from the British Library.

Papers used by Michael O'Mara Books Limited are natural, recyclable products made from wood grown in sustainable forests. The manufacturing processes conform to the environmental regulations of the country of origin.

ISBN: 978-1-78929-197-1 in hardback print format
ISBN: 978-1-78929-233-6 in trade paperback format
ISBN: 978-1-78929-198-8 in ebook format

1 2 3 4 5 6 7 8 9 10

Designed and typeset by Claire Cater
Maps by David Woodroffe
Illustrations by Aubrey Smith
Printed and bound by CPI Group (UK) Ltd, Croydon, CR0 4YY

www.mombooks.com

CONTENTS

· ✖ ·

INTRODUCTION

· ⟡ ·

Throughout human history, certain places have been the site of epochal events, a consistent focus of incident or a monument to tragedy. Others are perhaps, at first glance, less well known, but, in microcosm, detail a wider narrative about a long-term historical trend or theme. This extends across changes and developments in science, economics, religion, the arts and society. *A Short History of the World in 50 Places* contains all of these types of site, and more, offering a new narrative of humanity from its earliest phase to the twenty-first century.

This book, which is organized in chronological order, details the impact, legacy and role of fifty places that determined our history. It begins with the emergence of early humans in Africa, and the Olduvai Gorge in Tanzania, where some of our earliest ancestors began to master simple tools, the use of which enabled them to spread out across the world, and make their mark on every continent on our planet, from Australasia to the Americas. The book then moves on to the early ancient world, and the emergence of the first civilizations, such as those that emerged in the Fertile Crescent, the Nile valley and the Yellow River basin. The third chapter considers the later ancient world, and places such as the Temple Mount in Jerusalem, which became sacred to three faiths, and the Acropolis of Athens, which stands as a monument to the glories of the Greek Golden Age. Following from this, chapters four and five detail the medieval era, from the University of Timbuktu, one of the greatest centres of learning in the Islamic world, to Samarkand in modern-day Uzbekistan, a major stop on the Silk Road; and from Tenochtitlan in Mexico, the great centre of the Aztec Empire, to the Turkish Straits, one of the most strategically vital waterways in the world. Chapter six moves on to the early modern age; with places such as the parish of Belém telling the story of how Portugal, and other European nations, began the centuries-long process of empire-building, and Cape Coast Castle in Ghana, which became a central hub in the Atlantic slave trade. The series of revolutionary events that laid the foundations for the modern world is detailed in chapter seven, including New Lanark, the Scottish village that heralded the beginning of factory-based mechanized industry, and the house in Venezuela where Simón Bolívar and his confederates forged the future of independent Latin America. Finally, chapter eight considers the modern world, from Hollywood, where so much of the contemporary media landscape has been determined, to the Korean Demilitarized Zone, perhaps one of the last surviving symbols of the Cold War tensions that once appeared to have the world on the brink of nuclear annihilation.

Wherever and whenever your interests lie, *A Short History of the World in 50 Places* will give you new insights and perspectives into the past.

1

PREHISTORIC HISTORY

· ❧ ·

OLDUVAI GORGE

· ·

Around 2 million years ago the earliest humans emerged in sub-Saharan Africa. They have been classified as *Homo habilis* ('skilful man'). Over the millennia they evolved into modern humans, *Homo sapiens* ('wise man'), which settled across the world. Knowledge of our distant ancestors was made possible because of a series of discoveries at Olduvai Gorge in Tanzania.

On the eastern edge of the Serengeti Plain, the Olduvai Gorge is a steep ravine about 48 km (30 miles) long. Its name derives from *Oldupai*, which means 'place of the wild sisal' (a spiky plant common in the location) in the language of the local Maasai people. In prehistoric times it was next to a lake, meaning it was an important gathering place for animals and early humans. Their remains were well preserved due to ash-fall from nearby volcanos. In 1911, the scientist Wilhelm Kattwinkel (1866–1935) discovered fossil deposits (including

THE GREAT RIFT VALLEY

The East African Rift, which is about 6,400 km (4,000 miles) long, runs from the southernmost tip of Turkey to the mouth of the Zambezi in Mozambique. It began to be formed 30 million years ago as the Earth's crust pulled apart, creating valleys up to 80 km (50 miles) wide and 309 m (1,000 feet) deep, as well as numerous mountain ranges and lakes. It was in this diverse environment that apes evolved into modern humans, making it one of the most fossil-rich locations in the world.

the teeth of a *Hipparion*, a now-extinct ancient horse) in the gorge, which was then part of German East Africa. After he presented his finds in Berlin, a formal research expedition was sent there, led by the geologist and palaeontologist Hans Reck (1886–1937). By this time, the theory of evolution was well established, and it was widely accepted that humans had developed from primates. The fossil record to prove this evolution was incomplete, and there were still huge gaps in the understanding of how and where this process had taken place. At the time the oldest known hominid fossils to have been discovered were specimens of *Homo erectus* ('upright man') that had been found in Asia. Its ability to walk upright freed its hands to make tools and manipulate the environment. It had probably evolved from *Australopithecus*, a group of primate species. Reck's expedition found hundreds of animal fossils, as well as the complete skeleton of a *Homo sapiens*, which he claimed could be over 500,000 years old. This date was widely doubted, although it raised interest in the gorge and more expeditions to the site were planned (the scepticism proved to be well placed – later carbon dating revealed the skeleton to be just 17,000 years old). The First World War delayed further excavations at Olduvai, and they did not resume until 1931, by which time the area had come under the control of the British Empire.

The British expedition was led by the Kenyan-born palaeoanthropologist Louis Leakey (1903–72), who had earlier visited Reck in Germany and viewed the Oldowan fossils. He and his family would spend decades excavating the gorge, making a series of discoveries that revolutionized the understanding of early humans. Although Louis and his team, who included his wife Mary (1913–96), also a palaeoanthropologist, found well-worked hand-axes at Olduvai that were about 1 million years old, at first they did not find any hominid remains that pre-dated *Homo erectus*.

NEANDERTHALS

By around 400,000 years ago another species of hominid, distinct from *Homo sapiens*, had developed: *Homo neanderthalensis*. Their name derives from the Neander Valley in Germany, where the first specimen was found in 1856. From Europe, they spread out into North Africa and parts of Asia. Their shorter limbs, larger noses and stockier bodies allowed them to cope with the region's generally colder climate. Far from being ignorant cavemen, they probably used vocal language, mastered fire, and made tools out of flaked stone.

A major breakthrough came on 17 July 1959, on the Leakeys' seventh expedition to Olduvai. While Mary was walking her six Dalmatians she found a fragment of bone. It proved to be part of a mostly complete skull that was 1.75 million years old; it was nicknamed 'Nutcracker Man' because of its large molar teeth. The Leakeys determined that it belonged to a species of australopithecines, proving that humans evolved in Africa. The next year, Mary and Louis's son Jonathan (b. 1940) found the lower mandible and other parts of an early human in the gorge. After extensive study, and some further discoveries of similar remains, it was identified as the species that bridged the evolutionary gap between australopithecines and *Homo erectus.* In 1964, it was announced that the new species would be classified as *Homo habilis*, which means 'handy man'. It was discovered to have evolved between 2.4 and 1.5 million years ago and was so named because its larger brain gave it the ability to make more sophisticated tools.

The Olduvai Gorge also contained many examples of stone tools made by early humans. *Homo habilis*, who were probably hunters and scavengers, made tools through a technique known as 'knapping' – shaping stones by repeatedly striking them against other surfaces, thereby creating a sharp cutting edge. The Oldowan tools were mostly used for butchering animals and breaking their bones, allowing access to nutritious marrow. Tools were developed that could also be used to build shelters using branches, as well as to make wooden weapons and traps. The use of stone tools was vital to the flourishing of hominids because it allowed them to adjust to a wider variety of areas. Around 1.9 million years ago, *Homo habilis* evolved into *Homo erectus*, which used even more sophisticated stone tools and could control fire. Then, around 200,000 years ago, anatomically modern humans, *Homo sapiens*, emerged in East Africa. Fossils of both *Homo erectus* and *Homo sapiens* have also been found at Olduvai Gorge, meaning that it tells a story over 2 million years of how our species evolved from primates.

Homo sapiens did not remain in Africa. Their larger brains and greater intelligence gave them the ability to live in a wider range of environments, and they spread into the Near East between 130,000 and 100,000 years ago. Around 50,000 years ago they expanded into Europe and further into Asia.

After *Homo sapiens* arrived in these places there was probably interbreeding with Neanderthals. Genetic testing has shown that modern humans from these regions still carry Neanderthal DNA. However, *Homo neanderthalensis* as a distinct species became extinct approximately 40,000 years ago; the reasons for this are still debated, although possible causes include climate change or being supplanted by *Homo sapiens*.

JEBEL IRHOUD

In 1961, excavations started at a cave in Jebel Irhoud in western Morocco after a miner found a fossil skull of a *Homo sapiens* there. Further digs commenced in 2004, which uncovered more hominid remains, animal bones, evidence of fire and burned flint tools. The tools were around 315,000 years old, which makes the Jebel Irhoud fossils the oldest examples of anatomically modern humans.

By 15,000 years ago there were *Homo sapiens* living in almost every habitable corner of the world, including Australia and the Americas. At first *Homo sapiens* were hunter-gatherers (as were *Homo erectus*), living in small nomadic groups of between thirty and fifty people. They relied on hunting and scavenging wild animals as well as gathering naturally growing plants.

There was relative equality between men and women and, as these communities were constantly on the move, there was little opportunity to accumulate private property, which meant that Palaeolithic society was fairly egalitarian. Over time, *Homo sapiens* began to engage in ritual behaviour, with the first burials of the dead taking place 100,000 years ago and the first representative visual art being made about 50,000 years ago. More advanced tools were made, including the simple bow and arrow 14,000 years ago – in many ways this was the first machine, as it had moving parts and turned muscular energy into mechanical energy. This, along with other innovations like nets, spear throwers and bolas, allowed humans to hunt larger animals. This 'Old Stone Age' began to come to an end from around 10,000 BC, as humans, starting in the Middle East, began to transition into living in permanent agricultural societies.

LAKE MUNGO

. . . .

The Aboriginal Australians are the world's oldest civilization, with a continuous culture that goes back millennia. They reached Australia over 50,000 years ago, settling across the continent. The oldest fossil evidence of the Aborigines was found in Lake Mungo, a dried-up lake in south-western New South Wales.

In 1968, Jim Bowler, an Australian geologist studying ancient sand dunes, was in Lake Mungo and spotted what he thought were burned human bones that had been exposed to view by erosion. The next year he returned with archaeologists, who excavated the remains and took them in a suitcase to the Australian National University in Canberra for further study. They found that the fossilized bones were the remains of a young woman who was 1.47 m (4 feet 10 inches) tall. Her remains showed that she had been cremated and had her bones scattered with red ochre, which suggests that her culture engaged in ritual behaviour and possibly had some sense of an afterlife. In 1974, Bowler was riding his motorbike investigating the area in and around Lake Mungo when he caught sight of a bundle of human remains sticking out of a block of rock; it was excavated, taken to Canberra, and found to be an adult man who was 1.7 m (5 feet 7 inches) tall, aged about fifty, and had osteoarthritis in his right elbow (probably as the result of spear-throwing). He had lost two of his canine teeth at the same time when he was young, possibly in some kind of ritual ceremony. Both the 'Mungo Lady' and the 'Mungo Man' died around 42,000 years ago, at which point Australia was already widely settled by the Aborigines.

Studies of contemporary DNA suggest that the Aboriginal Australians are descendants of a group of *Homo sapiens* that left Africa around 72,000 years ago, migrating into South-East Asia before crossing into Australia. Some of the earliest evidence of human settlement was uncovered in Arnhem Land, northern Australia, where stone tools dating to between 53,000 and 61,000 years old were found in two rock shelters. From these first settlements, the Aborigines

AUSTRALIAN MEGAFAUNA

Australia's geographical isolation meant that the Aborigines encountered animals unknown elsewhere on Earth. Many of the species who lived there lacked natural predators before the arrival of humans, making them a ready source of food for the Aborigines. Species that may have been hunted into extinction include the Diprotodon, a marsupial the size of a hippopotamus, and the Genyornis, a flightless bird that was over 1.8 m (6 feet) tall.

migrated across the whole of the continent by 35,000 years ago. They largely retained the hunter-gatherer lifestyle that characterized early human societies (although some groups practised a form of agriculture, with evidence of harvesting and storage of plants, as well as elaborate systems to trap eels and fish). They were skilled trackers and stalkers, and masters of the spear-thrower. Fire was vital to their existence, used for cooking, and to drive animals out of their burrows; the resulting ashes acted as a fertilizer, helping plants to regrow.

Many features of the Australian landscape at the time of the first human settlement there were different from today's. When the Aborigines first arrived in Lake Mungo between 50,000 and 45,000 years ago, it was part of an inland region containing thirteen large freshwater lakes that had been filled as a result of a gradually cooling climate, which led to less evaporation. In addition to lakes, there was grassland and woods teeming with wildlife. Around 40,000 years ago, dust storms blew in sand from upwind dunes, and rising temperatures reduced the water levels. Lake Mungo dried up 19,000 years ago, and people moved to other areas in the vicinity that had a more reliable water supply.

The Aboriginal Australians divided themselves into over 500 tribes, each of which was linked to a specific ancestral area. Although there was no system of writing, there was a complex system of myth passed on orally down the generations. Nor was there much in the way of social hierarchy (although elders had status due to their knowledge of tribal lore – it generally took thirty to forty years to learn the full cycle of myth, including songs, dances and sacred sites). Despite the fact that there were over 300 different Aboriginal languages and sporadic violence between different groups, there was widespread cultural exchange. Neighbouring tribes often gathered together for ceremonial events and there were trade networks that stretched inland from the coast for over 1,600 km (1,000 miles). As they were largely nomadic, the Aborigines produced little in the way of permanent habitation. An exception was in south-west Victoria, where 600 years ago they built huts that could house families of four to seven that were lived in for part of the year. Being almost constantly on the move kept population densities low; by the end of the eighteenth century there were just 300,000 Aborigines living in Australia, meaning the population density was just one person in every 26 square km (10 square miles).

BOTANY BAY

On 29 April 1770, HMS *Endeavour*, captained by James Cook, landed in eastern Australia, having charted islands in the South Pacific and navigated New Zealand's coastline. The British named the site Botany Bay, and then charted 8,000 km (5,000 miles) of Australian coastline before returning home. In 1788, a British fleet carrying 1,030 people (including 736 convicts) landed at Botany Bay. Finding it to be an unsuitable site for a penal colony, they moved 8 km (5 miles) north to found Port Jackson, which grew into Sydney.

In 1786, the British government decided to settle Australia with convicts, with the First Fleet arriving two years later. By the end of the eighteenth century, there were over 5,000 colonists living in Australia. Over the course of the nineteenth and twentieth century, millions more migrants arrived. Britain had taken control of the land merely by proclaiming its sovereignty over it, without making any treaties with the indigenous population. This was possible thanks to a legal theory that they were claiming *terra nullius* – land that was vacant and belonged to no one. The rights of the Aborigines were completely ignored – it was not until 1992 that an Australian legal decision recognized that they had owned and possessed their ancestral territory. The process of colonization has been disastrous and traumatic for Aboriginal society – in addition to the loss of their lands, they suffered from Western diseases and violence at the hands of settlers.

The bones of the Mungo Lady and Mungo Man remained in Canberra for decades, having been taken there without the permission of the three tribes, the Paakantyi, Muthi Muthi and Ngiyampaa, who are recognized as the traditional owners of the area. Following negotiations with the tribes, the Mungo Lady's bones were returned in 1992. They are kept in a locked safe in the Mungo National Park exhibition centre, which needs two keys to open: one is held by archaeologists, one by the tribal elders. However, it took until 2017 for the Mungo Man to be repatriated – he was eventually reburied on the edge of Lake Mungo. His bones will now remain in the earth where they had once lain undisturbed for centuries.

2

THE EARLY
ANCIENT WORLD

· · ❧ · ·

THE FERTILE CRESCENT
. . . .

Around 12,000 years ago, some human cultures began to
shift from nomadic hunter-gatherer societies to permanent
agricultural settlements. This 'Neolithic Revolution' transformed
the world; allowing larger populations, greater specialization
and the emergence of the first towns and cities.

The Fertile Crescent is a region in the Middle East defined
by two major rivers, the Tigris and Euphrates, which originate
in the mountains of Turkey and Iran and flow into the Persian
Gulf, together providing a crucial supply of fresh water. The best
farmland was in the area known as Mesopotamia, between the
two rivers, where farming had begun by 9000 BC. In the Fertile
Crescent grew wild cereal grasses that could be domesticated
and farmed, such as emmer wheat, barley, millet and flax, as

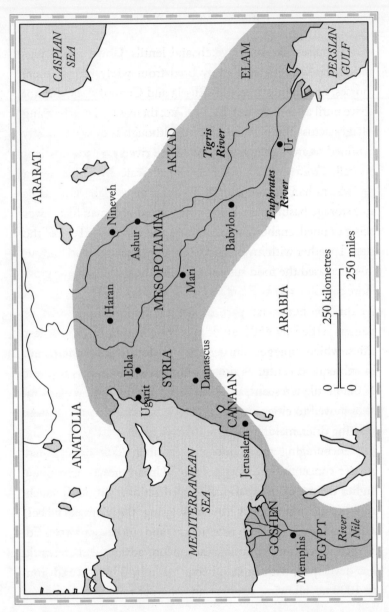

The Fertile Crescent, c. sixth millenium BC

well as pulses like bitter vetch and lentils. Cows, goats, pigs and sheep were all selectively bred from wild animals there (horses, first domesticated in Russia and Central Asia, did not arrive until after 4000 BC). By 7000 BC, there were large farming villages across the Fertile Crescent, although they were mostly confined to areas that were close to the rivers or had sufficient rainfall. From around 6000 BC, small-scale irrigation using the waters had begun, and by 5000 BC more elaborate canals and storage basins were being constructed and marshland was being drained, enabling more intense and widespread use of the land. Together with inventions like the seed plough and harrow, this increased the food supply, allowing the population to grow more rapidly.

The southernmost part of Mesopotamia was known as Sumer; settled by 4500 BC, it was the location of the earliest cities, which emerged during the mid-fourth millennium BC. In subsequent centuries urbanization extended across the rest of the Fertile Crescent, and into Persia and Egypt. People may have moved to cities around this time because the climate was growing drier, making subsistence agriculture harder to sustain and encouraging more intensive farming, which demanded greater concentration of population. Urban growth allowed a higher degree of occupational specialization, with crafts such as weaving and pottery (by now using the potter's wheel, which allowed quicker production and more sophisticated designs) becoming commonplace. More advanced metalwork was developed, with bronze being made by 3500 BC and iron by 1000 BC, allowing stronger and sharper tools and weapons.

Despite the existence of these crafts, most of the population still worked in agriculture, walking out to their fields from their homes within cities. The Fertile Crescent established long-distance trade; wheeled vehicles were in widespread use by 3000 BC, meaning heavy goods could be transported long distances. By this time, Mesopotamians were building boats large enough to haul goods, and by 2300 BC they were trading as far afield as Oman and India. Despite their sophisticated economy, the cultures of the Fertile Crescent did not use coinage; payments were generally bartered and wages were mostly paid in grain, which was measured using standardized weights.

The cities of the Fertile Crescent grew into states that controlled a surrounding area of about 16 km (10 miles), containing farmland and villages. Political hierarchies emerged – at first these city-states were ruled by assemblies of their leading men, but from 3000 BC they were largely supplanted by individual rulers who eventually established hereditary monarchies. The first ruler for whom there is archaeological evidence (his name appears on remnants of an alabaster vase) is Enmebaragesi, who ruled the Sumerian city-state of Kish in around 2500 BC. The primary role of these early kings was to provide military leadership, as the growing city-states developed rivalries and began to fight for influence and territory. The first battle in recorded human history (depicted in a carving on a limestone monument) was fought around 2450 BC between the two Sumerian cities of Lagash and Umma over control of an area of irrigated land. Lagash emerged victorious, with their king, Eannatum, recorded as personally leading his men to triumph despite being struck by an arrow. Kings also kept order and oversaw projects like the construction of city walls, irrigation systems and granaries (some were very large – in the city of Shuruppak there was enough barley stored to feed its population of 20,000 for six months). Organized religions emerged; each city-state generally had its own patron gods and elaborate temple complexes devoted to them; from 2000 BC a common structure was the ziggurat, a large stepped pyramid that symbolized sacred mountains. Kings encouraged links with religion, claiming their rule was divinely ordained and incorporating religious ceremonies in state functions.

CUNEIFORM

From around 3300 BC, the Sumerians developed the first system of writing – cuneiform. It was written with a bevel-tipped reed on tablets of wet clay that were baked hard, and at first it was a limited set of pictograms used to keep track of goods, crops and taxes. Within 600 years it had evolved into a system of 1,000 phonetic symbols, which could be used to write literary works. The system was eventually adopted across the Middle East, and was in use as late as the first century AD.

The Fertile Crescent was home to the first emperor in history – Sargon, who was born in the twenty-fourth century BC in the Sumerian city of Kish. The son of a gardener, he became the cup-bearer of the King of Kish before overthrowing him and seizing power. In order to project his authority, he took the regnal name Sharru-kin, meaning 'the king is legitimate.' From 2334 BC, he began to conquer all of Mesopotamia, and he founded a new imperial capital named Akkad (probably located on the site of present-day Baghdad). In the city-states Sargon conquered, he allowed the original rulers to stay in place, although they were now provincial governors who ruled at his pleasure. He had a standing army of over 5,000, enacted a system of centralized taxation, where money was sent to him, and gave land to his supporters. Sargon's successors extended his realms but they also faced numerous local rebellions, as well as invasions from Persia, Syria and Anatolia. The Akkadian Empire collapsed in 2154 BC, and the area it covered reverted to its previous system of independent city-states.

After the fall of the Akkadian Empire, the next great power to rise in the Fertile Crescent was Babylon, which was established as a city-state on the banks of the Euphrates in 1894 BC. Under the rule of Hammurabi, which lasted from 1792 to 1750 BC, Babylon conquered surrounding city-states to establish dominance over much of Mesopotamia. Hammurabi was an energetic ruler eager to extend his authority. His code of law, promulgated around 1754 BC, is the oldest such document to survive. It was recorded on a 2.3-metre-high (almost 8 feet) column of black diorite stone; numerous copies were made that were placed across the Babylonian Empire, displayed prominently in public squares and temples. The code contained 282 judgments concerning a range of subjects including slavery, commerce, wages, adultery, marriage and adoption. A guiding principle was 'an eye for an eye', a concept that was highly influential on other legal codes and religions – for example, in the Old Testament. After Hammurabi died, his empire disintegrated, although Babylon remained a great centre of learning, religion and commerce. By this stage, the innovations made in the Fertile Crescent had already spread out, and been established for centuries, across Asia and into Africa and Europe, making it one of the most influential civilizations in human history.

THE NILE

The longest river in the world, the Nile flows over 6,400 km (4,000 miles) through Africa into the Mediterranean. Without its life-giving waters, three millennia of Ancient Egyptian civilization would have been impossible, and it has played a central role in shaping the region's past, present and future.

In Egypt the Nile acts as an oasis that runs through the Sahara Desert. It has two main parts: the Valley, which is about 13 km (8 miles) wide, and the Delta, a series of lagoons and swamps 240 km (150 miles) wide that branches out onto the Mediterranean coast, enabling easy sea links between Egypt and Europe. The

Nile has two main sources (although their precise locations were not fully established until the later nineteenth century): Lake Tana in Ethiopia and Lake Victoria in East Africa, with the former flowing into the Blue Nile (so-called because of the clay carried in the water) and the latter into the White Nile. The two sections meet in modern-day Sudan, just north of the capital, Khartoum.

PYRAMIDS

Pyramids were monumental burial complexes for the pharaohs and their families. They originated from the step pyramid built for Djoser around 2650 BC near Memphis. These developed into smooth-sided pyramids; the largest ever was at Giza for Khufu, who reigned in the twenty-sixth century BC; it rose to nearly 152 m (500 feet) and covered an area of thirteen acres. Without the Nile, the pyramids would have been impossible; construction materials (and sustenance for the workforce) were transported to the building sites by channels cut from the river.

In an otherwise mostly waterless region, the Nile was so vital that the Ancient Egyptians simply called it *Itrw*, meaning 'the River' ('Nile' is derived from the Ancient Greek name,

Neilos). The Nile enabled the first farming settlements to arise along its banks (in modern-day Egypt) after around 5000 BC. This allowed the cultivation of barley, wheat, flax, fruit and vegetables, as well as the keeping of livestock. In addition, a species of aquatic plant called *Cyperus papyrus* grew wild along the Nile. Its pith was used to make papyrus, a thick paper-like material used as a writing surface by the Egyptians and other ancient peoples. A further factor in the Nile's importance was that it reliably flooded every year. During the late summer it broke its banks, depositing a rich layer of silt, fertilizing the soil and washing out salts. The Ancient Egyptians called the annual flooding of the Nile *Akhet*, and believed it was caused by the tears of the goddess Isis weeping for her dead husband Osiris. The true cause of the inundation, though, was monsoon rainfall hundreds of miles upriver in Ethiopia, which caused a surge in the volume of water that eventually led to flooding of the Nile in Egypt. The floodwaters sat in natural basins that formed an immense reservoir of water for farming during the six to eight weeks when the river was in flood. These natural basins were added to by a complex system of dykes and irrigation canals that allowed the water to be stored and distributed more effectively.

The Nile no longer annually floods in Egypt. Since the mid-nineteenth century, a series of increasingly ambitious projects have transformed the flow of the river, beginning with dams and sluices that were built to create irrigation canals that allowed a year-round supply of water. These culminated in the Aswan High Dam, which was initiated by Gamal Abdel

Nasser (1918–70), who became President of Egypt in 1956. He hoped that the dam would stimulate and modernize the Egyptian economy. When the American and British governments withdrew their funding for the dam (partly as a result of Nasser's policy of trying to maintain neutrality during the Cold War), he decided to help pay for it by nationalizing the Suez Canal, which had been owned by a corporation that had been in the hands of the French and British governments. Despite the resulting Suez Crisis, Nasser, and Egypt, retained control of the canal and used the tolls to build the dam between 1960 and 1970. Nasser, who remained president during this period, died of a heart attack just two months after the dam was completed. The dam created Lake Nasser (which extends into Sudan, where it is called Lake Nubia), a man-made reservoir that allowed the Egyptian authorities to control the flooding of the Nile to provide a more reliable water supply for agriculture, and generate electricity using hydropower.

The final major function of the ancient Nile was as a transportation route for goods and people. The earliest craft that plied its waters were small rafts made of reeds that were platforms for fishermen. Over time these developed into large pleasure vessels and huge barges that could transport bulky goods like granite or grain. In Egypt, the Nile was mostly easy to navigate; its speed was a leisurely one knot, rising to four knots when it was in flood. Prevailing winds meant it was possible to sail north, but travelling south, upstream, required oar-power. On the Nile outside of Egypt, navigation was hindered by the river's six 'cataracts', sections where rocks and stones stick up

THE SUEZ CANAL

The Suez Canal opened in 1869, allowing ships to sail from the Mediterranean to the Indian Ocean without having to go around Africa, making it one of the most important waterways in the world. The United Kingdom militarily seized the canal in 1882 and established a protectorate over Egypt. In 1956, Nasser nationalized the canal to finance building of the Aswan High Dam. In response, British, French and Israeli forces invaded Egypt to regain control of the canal. Under international pressure, they withdrew, and the Egyptian government regained control of the waterway.

out of the water; this disrupts the flow and creates rapids. North of the Elephantine, an island near the First Cataract, there are no impediments to ships and boats for about 1,200 km (750 miles), allowing easy travel all the way to the Mediterranean.

The first Egyptian state is traditionally believed to have started around 3100 BC. The various city-states along the Nile were unified by the semi-legendary ruler Menes (now widely identified as being a local king called Narmer), founder of the First Dynasty. He and his successors became known by the title 'Pharaoh', which derives from the Egyptian for 'great house'. The pharaohs were also known as the 'Lords of Two

Lands', because they ruled both Lower Egypt (centred on the Nile Delta) and Upper Egypt (the Nile valley). Therefore, an important symbol of their power was the double crown, with the white part representing Lower Egypt and the red standing for Upper Egypt. Over the centuries, the pharaohs developed an increasingly centralized administrative structure, centred on their capital of Memphis, which occupied a strategic position near the apex of the Nile Delta.

JEBEL SAHABA

The oldest evidence of human conflict is an ancient cemetery at Jebel Sahaba, on the east bank of the Nile in northern Sudan. The site, which is 13,000 years old, was the burial place of sixty-one hunter-gatherers. Around half had died violently, with marks suggesting they had been attacked with spears or arrows. They may have been involved in a struggle for access to the Nile.

The pharaohs regarded their 'natural' territory as extending from the Elephantine to the Delta. However, there were frequent incursions south of the Elephantine into the region of Nubia, which was mostly located in modern-day Sudan. Although the Nubian part of the Nile was not as fertile as the Egyptian section, it was economically important as a route for caravans carrying spices, ivory, ebony and precious metals. Furthermore, the pharaohs recruited heavily for their police and armed forces in the region. In around 1500 BC, the Egyptians launched a full-scale invasion of Nubia, conquering it and adding it to their empire. Nubia remained under Egyptian rule until the eleventh century BC, when it broke away. To the north of the Nile, from the sixteenth to eleventh century BC, Egypt expanded its power across the Sinai Desert and into the Middle East, fighting with the Hittite Empire (which was based in Anatolia) for control of Syria and Canaan.

By the ninth century BC, the power of the Egyptian pharaohs was fragmenting; there was internal disorder, and they had lost influence in Asia and were facing incursions from foreign powers. Indeed, both the Kingdom of Kush, a powerful state in Nubia, and the Neo-Assyrian Empire, which originated in Mesopotamia, conquered some or all of Egypt at various times. The final defeat came in 525 BC, at the hands of the Persian Achaemenid Empire, which following victory at the Battle of Pelusium, on the eastern part of the Nile Delta, captured Memphis. Egypt became a Persian province, although the Achaemenids ruled there in the guise of a pharaoh, adopting his titles. Aside from a period of native rule between 404 and 343 BC, Persian rule lasted until 332 BC, when Egypt was conquered by Alexander the Great (356–323 BC). Egypt was then ruled or dominated by a succession of foreign powers, including the Romans, Byzantines, Arabs, Ottomans and British, until it established itself as an independent republic in 1953.

THE YELLOW RIVER BASIN

During the Stone Age, the earliest Chinese civilizations emerged along the middle section of the Yellow River (*Huang He*). This part of the river runs through the North China Plain, which was the home of the Xia, believed to be the first of the dynasties to rule the country.

The Yellow River, which is 5,464 km (3,395 miles) long, originates in the Bayan Har Mountains and runs to the Bohai Sea on China's north-eastern coast. It gained its name because of its yellow colour, which is caused by the volume of sedimentation (the highest of any river in the world) that discharges sand and mud into its waters. This means that the Yellow River can often be difficult to navigate, because of shifting sand banks. In addition, the river frequently breaks its banks (1,500 times in the last 2,500 years), leading to floods that give it its nickname, 'China's Sorrow'. Even more seriously, the river has been known to shift its course dramatically due to silt building up in the riverbed, which leads to the waters shifting. This would have been catastrophic for the ancient Chinese people whose homes would have been destroyed – in addition it would have destroyed evidence of many Stone Age and Bronze Age sites. Despite this, the Yellow River is still viewed as the cradle of civilization in China. This is because when the river floods and recedes it leaves behind layers of silt that enrich the soil, meaning that it creates fertile land ideal for agriculture.

Farming in China began along the Yellow River, during the seventh and sixth millennia BC, at a time when climate change made the area warm and wet, and small villages emerged where crops like millet and rice were cultivated. By the second millennium BC, the North China Plain was becoming increasingly densely populated and urbanized, with thousands of walled city-states emerging in the region. Each was ruled by its own chief, and there was frequent warfare, leading to some city-states gaining dominance over others. It was in this political landscape that the first dynasty in Chinese traditional history emerged: the Xia.

The origin of the Xia dynasty, which emerged around 2100 BC, is inextricably bound to the Yellow River. The first Xia king was Yu, whose father was Gun, who had attempted to control the river's waters by spending years building dykes out of magic soil stolen from the gods. At first Gun's dykes worked, magically rising at the same time as the water until they eventually collapsed, causing harmful floods. For his theft, the gods executed Gun (some sources suggest he committed suicide). Yu was determined to succeed where his father had failed – instead of damming the Yellow River (and other waterways in the region), he spent a decade dredging it and building irrigation canals, allowing its waters to drain away peacefully. As a result Yu was made king. Scholars question whether Yu actually existed; there is no contemporary evidence for him, as writing had not been developed in China when he was said to have lived. However, the account of his life may have been based on orally transmitted stories of how rulers attempted to battle the cataclysmic flooding

of the Yellow River, and he has become regarded as the archetype of a wise and virtuous ruler.

Yu was so beloved that the people allowed his son Qi to succeed him, setting the tradition for hereditary rule and establishing the Xia dynasty. It lasted until around 1600 BC, when its tyrannical and dissolute final ruler, Jie, was overthrown by Tang, a local king, who established the Shang dynasty. Whether or not the Xia dynasty truly existed, what is certain is that Shang rule, for which there is documentary evidence, represented a transition towards greater levels of political organization. The Shang dynasty expanded their power out from the Yellow River valley to cover a wider area of north-eastern China. They developed a sophisticated administration, issuing edicts to local governors, and building elaborate palace complexes and royal tombs. During this era the earliest known Chinese writing was developed, a system of over 2,000 pictographs. It has been most commonly discovered inscribed on animal bones or shells used by oracles to divine the future (they would carve their questions and then apply heat with a metal rod and interpret the cracks that formed). In *c.* 1046 BC, a ruler called Wu of Zhou overthrew the final Shang king, Shou, who was said to be an immoral and sadistic drunkard. Wu defeated Shou's armies, forcing him to retreat to his palace in the city of Yin, where he committed suicide. The Zhou legitimized their rebellion and seizure of power by arguing that the Shang had lost the 'Mandate of Heaven', the powers to govern that were granted to rulers by the gods. This progression through the Xia, Shang and Zhou dynasties as rulers of China is attested to in many ancient sources but in reality it may not have been so simple – it is a possibility that they all existed at the same time (along with many other small states in the Yellow River Plain) but conquered each other's territory.

THE INDUS VALLEY CIVILIZATION

The first South Asian civilization arose in the basin of the Indus River, in modern-day north-eastern Afghanistan, Pakistan and north-western India. Agriculture was established there by the end of the fourth millennium BC, with urban settlements by 2500 BC. The civilization came to an end by around 1700 BC, when a combination of invasions, drought and earthquakes led to the decay and abandonment of most of its cities.

By the first millennium BC, the Chinese state had extended its power beyond its heartland along the Yellow River. However, it remained crucial as a source of water for agriculture. During the early seventh century AD, it was linked to the Yangtze, the main river in southern China (which unlike the Yellow River, very rarely flooded), by the Grand Canal, which economically and politically integrated the country. Although there were numerous attempts to control it through levees and dykes, the Yellow River still periodically floods, often causing thousands of deaths. From the mid-twentieth century, there have been several ambitious attempts to harness and control the river's power by building hydroelectric dams and flood-control systems, which will hopefully mean it no longer brings sorrow to China.

NAURU

. . . .

One of the greatest feats in human history was the settlement of Oceania by its indigenous peoples. The arrival of Europeans in the eighteenth and nineteenth century transformed the region; the story of the island of Nauru displays the sometimes tragic consequences of this meeting of cultures.

Oceania is comprised of four cultural and geographical regions: Australasia, Melanesia, Micronesia and Polynesia. The first to be settled by humans was Melanesia, when the Papuan people migrated to New Guinea over 40,000 years ago. It was not until around 3000 BC that they, together with

The regions of Oceania

Austronesians from South-East Asia, pushed further east into the smaller islands of Melanesia. The islands in the area to the north, known as Micronesia, were settled by 1000 BC, and around 2,000 years ago there was another wave of migration further east, to Polynesia. These long-distance voyages between islands were made across the vast expanse of the Pacific Ocean, using outrigger canoes that sailed for weeks across the open sea without instruments like sextants or compasses. Rather, navigating was carried out by observing changes and movements in celestial bodies, the waves and even birds.

WAITANGI

The last major land mass to be settled by humans was New Zealand, whose indigenous peoples, the Māori, arrived in the thirteenth century. Dutch explorers visited in 1642, but it was the British who colonized it. In 1838, the British government decided to annexe it, and began negotiations with Māori chiefs in Waitangi. A treaty was signed on 6 February 1840. The signatories accepted the sovereignty of Queen Victoria (1819–1901), who had the sole right to purchase their lands and guaranteed their rights as British subjects. The treaty's implementation remains controversial, as it has been repeatedly violated.

Nauru is an oval-shaped island, just 21 square km (8 square miles) in size, surrounded by a coral reef. It is located in the south-western Pacific Ocean, about 320 km (200 miles) from the nearest island. This meant it became a haven for seabirds, and over the centuries their droppings built up, leaching into the rocks and leaving a rich deposit of phosphates on the central plateau that rises to 30 metres (100 feet) above sea level. The substance would eventually radically transform the fate of the island. By around two millennia ago, Nauru had been settled, possibly by a mixture of Melanesians, Micronesians and Polynesians. Although interaction between other Pacific islands was commonplace, the people of Nauru were relatively isolated and self-contained – strong currents made deep-sea voyages difficult, so they mostly stayed close to their home.

On 8 November 1798, the British whaling ship *Hunter* sighted the island but did not land any men, although some Nauruan canoes paddled out to meet it. Despite this brief contact, the ship's captain, John Fearn, was left with a favourable enough impression to name the land 'Pleasant Island'. By the 1830s, whaling ships were using Nauru as a resupply point. At this time the first European residents arrived – they were 'beachcombers', i.e. deserters from ships or escaped convicts who settled in islands across the Pacific. Europeans brought with them alcohol, firearms and Western diseases; such rapid changes destabilized Nauruan society. During the 1870s, a young chief was accidentally shot at a marriage celebration. This led to over a decade of civil war between Nauru's twelve clans, now armed with guns, that may have killed a third of the population. In a bid to bring order to the island (and add to its burgeoning empire) Germany declared a protectorate over it in 1888. The gunboat SMS *Eber* was sent to the island, and thirty-six troops came ashore. They held all the chiefs under house arrest until all of the guns and ammunition had been turned over. German imperial authorities then banned the importation of alcohol and encouraged the arrival of Christian missionaries.

During the later nineteenth century, scientists discovered that phosphate rock could be processed to make a very efficient fertilizer. When it was realized that there were phosphate deposits on islands in the Pacific, Western nations began mining and quarrying phosphates on them. At first Nauru was excluded, but this would change. In 1899, Albert Ellis, who worked in the phosphates division of the Pacific Islands Company, noticed a strange-looking rock that one of his colleagues had brought back from Nauru and was using as a doorstop in their offices in Sydney, believing that it was fossilized wood. Ellis found that it was in fact phosphate ore, and his company began mining in Nauru the next year, with annual output quickly reaching 91,000 million kg (89,000 tonnes). Soon after the First World War started in 1914, Australian troops captured Nauru. After the conflict ended, the island was placed under a League of Nations mandate, with Australia, New Zealand and the United Kingdom as its trustees (in practice, the Australians took charge of the administration). Phosphate mining continued, with the Nauruans receiving only a small share of the profits.

The Second World War subjected Nauru to further depredation; in 1940, German cruisers bombarded the island,

and in 1942 it was conquered by Japan. The Japanese built an airstrip on Nauru and transported 1,200 people from there to work as forced labourers at Chuuk Lagoon, which was over 1,900 km (1,200 miles) away (only around half survived to be repatriated). Allied aircraft regularly bombed Nauru, which was not retaken from the Japanese until 1945. After the war, Nauru was made a United Nations trust territory, with the administrative arrangement from before the conflict re-established, and phosphate mining continuing. In 1968, Nauru won independence, becoming one of the smallest nations in the world. Phosphate continued to be extracted, and for a brief period Nauru had the highest GDP per capita on Earth. The government established a trust fund for their profits, making property investments across the world. However, as phosphate deposits were depleted and global prices fell, Nauru's economy faltered. To make matters worse, the government trust fund made a series of disastrous investments, including a failed London musical based on the life of Leonardo da Vinci (1452–1519).

By the early twenty-first century, with no phosphate left to mine, Nauru was in crisis. The mining had left a third of the island devastated, with scientists estimating it would take 1,000 years to restore biodiversity. The Nauruan government was effectively bankrupt; its assets had been seized and it was no longer able to fulfil its financial obligations. Searching for another source of revenue, in 2001 Nauru agreed with the Australian government to hold asylum seekers (mostly Afghani and Iraqi) for them. They remained on Nauru until 2008. Four years later, the Australian government reopened its offshore detention centre on Nauru, which has become as central to the island's economy as phosphate mining was. However, there has been international outcry at the treatment the refugees on Nauru receive, with reports of inhumane conditions and abuse. Although there are plans to conduct deep-sea mining off the Nauruan coast, the long-term future of the nation remains uncertain.

3

THE LATER ANCIENT WORLD

· ❊ ·

THE TEMPLE MOUNT

Jerusalem is sacred to three religions: Judaism, Christianity and Islam. Perhaps the holiest place in the city is the Temple Mount; the site of Solomon's Temple and the location of Muhammad's ascension to heaven.

Few places have been more fiercely battled for than Jerusalem, which began as a small village around 3000 BC. Located in the ancient region of Canaan, which extended across Palestine and Syria, it was named after one of the Canaanite deities, Shalem. In around 1000 BC, Jerusalem was conquered by David, who established it as the capital of his Kingdom of Israel. The Israelites had originated as pastoral nomads in Canaan, living in Egypt and Mesopotamia before returning to their homeland. Their religion, Judaism, was monotheistic, and was founded by the patriarch Abraham. Even before David's conquest of Jerusalem, the Temple Mount had played an important role in Judaism; many believed it was the location of 'Mount Moriah', where God ordered Abraham to prove his faith by sacrificing his first-born son, Isaac. When He saw Abraham had been willing to carry out his order, God commanded him to stop and a ram was sacrificed instead. Furthermore, the Temple Mount was the location of the 'Foundation Stone', from which Jews believed the world was created. David's son and successor, Solomon, built the First Temple on the site. At its centre was a small chamber called the Holy of Holies, which housed the sacred Ark of the Covenant, a gold-covered chest that contained the stone tablets on which Moses had carved the Ten Commandments. It had previously been housed in the Tabernacle, a multicoloured tent that David had erected. After Solomon's death in *c.* 930 BC, Israel was divided. The northern part, which retained the name Israel, was conquered by the Assyrians in 722 BC. The southern part, called Judah and containing Jerusalem, was taken by the Babylonians in 586 BC. They sacked Jerusalem, destroyed the First Temple and exiled much of the population to Babylon.

The Achaemenid Persian Empire conquered Babylon in 538 BC and allowed the captive Jews to return home. They were led by Zerubbabel, a member of the royal house of Judah, who acted as the governor of Jerusalem for the Persians. He oversaw the building of the Second Temple, which was completed in 516 BC. Jerusalem remained under Persian rule until the early fourth century BC, when it became part of Alexander the Great's empire.

HEROD'S TEMPLE

Herod completely reshaped the Temple Mount. He started by increasing the size of the plateau at its summit, doubling its area to around 36 acres. Herod then began extensive remodelling of the Temple itself. To ensure that religious ceremonies were not interrupted, he had the stones carved to size off-site so they could be slotted into place more quietly. He trained 1,000 priests as masons and carpenters to carry out work on the holiest parts of the Temple.

It remained under Greek control until the rebellion of the Maccabees, who opposed foreign interference and revolted from 167 to 160 BC. They re-established Judea's sovereignty, and Jerusalem became the capital of an independent kingdom ruled by the Jewish Hasmonean dynasty. In 63 BC the Roman Republic invaded Judea. Led by the general and politician Pompey (106–48 BC), they besieged Jerusalem, focusing their attack on the Temple Mount. Pompey used the Sabbath day to fill defensive ditches and build ramps for his siege engines, confident that the religious beliefs of the inhabitants precluded them from resisting him. He then advanced on the Temple Mount, even entering the Holy of Holies (a highly sacred area – indeed, many Jews today will not walk on the Temple Mount at all for fear of stepping on its location). After this Roman victory, the Hasmoneans ruled as client-kings until 37 BC, when they were overthrown by Herod (73–4 BC), a Jewish official who was a close ally of Rome. That year, Herod's forces, reinforced by Roman legions, captured Jerusalem. He then initiated extensive rebuilding and remodelling of the Temple Mount; the process lasted for eighty years.

Judea and Jerusalem came under direct Roman rule in AD 6. In around AD 30, a religious teacher called Jesus of Nazareth began preaching and attracting followers. At the time, tensions were high between Rome and its Jewish subjects and Jesus was seen as a potential threat to imperial authority (not helped by acts such as clearing the area around the Second Temple of the merchants and money changers who had gathered there). As a result, Jesus was crucified in Jerusalem in around 33, on the orders of the Roman provincial governor. This did not stop his disciples spreading the message that Jesus was humanity's saviour and the Son of God. At first the vast majority of Christians were Jewish people in Judea, but after the mid-first century people from other communities and areas began to convert, and Christianity eventually grew into the most widely followed faith in the world.

A rebellion against Roman rule swept Judea in 66. Four years later, Roman troops entered Jerusalem after a siege, destroying the Second Temple; all that remained were some retaining walls, foundations, vaults and the base of a tower. No Third Temple has been built, although its construction remains a cherished and sacred goal for many Jews. In 130, a Roman colony, Aelia Capitolina, was established on the site of Jerusalem and a temple dedicated to Jupiter was built on the Temple Mount. This angered many Jews, leading to further revolts. After these were defeated, Jews were forbidden to enter Jerusalem. This restriction was reversed in 363 under Julian (331/2–363), the last pagan emperor of Rome, who allowed his Jewish subjects to raise a small synagogue on the Temple Mount and then decided to build a Third Temple as part of his plans to encourage non-Christian religions. Fire (and possibly Christian hostility) prevented Julian carrying out his plans, and he died later that year.

The Temple Mount's link to Islam was established around 620 when the Prophet Muhammad (c. 570–632) was said to have made a miraculous journey, travelling to Jerusalem from Mecca in a single night astride a winged creature called Buraq ('Lightning'). On the Temple Mount, Muhammad met with Abraham, Moses and Jesus and led them in prayer, before ascending to heaven. As a result, Muslims know the Temple Mount as Haram al-Sharif ('Noble Sanctuary'). After Muhammad died, the Arab Caliphate rose to become one of the greatest powers in the Middle East. In 638, Caliph Umar (*c.* 584–644) entered Jerusalem, ending the Byzantine Empire's control of the city. He personally cleared the Temple compound, which had fallen into disrepair, carrying away the accumulated detritus and wreckage in his cloak. He initiated the construction of the Dome of the Rock, a shrine at the centre of the Temple Mount that marked Abraham's altar and where Muhammad had made his 'Night Journey'. It was completed in 691, as was a nearby prayer-house, the Dome of the Chain. The largest Muslim structure on the Temple Mount is the al-Aqsa Mosque; completed in 705, it was twice destroyed by earthquakes in 746 and 1033, but rebuilt each time.

THE KNIGHTS TEMPLAR

To help defend the Crusader states and Christian pilgrims, several military orders were established in the Holy Land. The most powerful were the Knights Templar, founded in Jerusalem in 1119, who remained influential until their suppression in 1312. They used the al-Aqsa Mosque as their headquarters, while the Dome of the Rock was converted into a church, with its Quranic inscriptions replaced by Latin texts and a cross replacing the crescent.

In 1095, Byzantium lobbied Pope Urban II (*c.* 1035–99) for help in its wars against the Muslim Seljuq Turks, who had conquered Palestine and much of Anatolia. This had disrupted the Christian pilgrimage route to the Holy Land, and so Urban called on the faithful to fight against the Turks. Many rallied to his cry, and the First Crusade set out in 1096. Rather than help Byzantium, they advanced into Palestine and in 1099 captured Jerusalem, sacking the city and massacring thousands. The victorious Crusaders then established their own states in the Holy Land, the most powerful of which was the Kingdom of Jerusalem. Muslim dominance of Palestine was re-established by Saladin (1137/8–93), a Kurdish soldier who established himself as ruler of Egypt in 1171. He then gained territory in Syria, Arabia and Mesopotamia before turning his attention to the Crusader states. In 1187, he captured Jerusalem, and reduced the Crusader territory to a small coastal strip that they would abandon by the end of the thirteenth century. When Saladin entered Jerusalem, he tore down the cross over the Dome of the Rock, and joined by family members and nobles, he scrubbed its floors with rose water. Although Jerusalem reverted to Christian rule between 1229 and 1244, the city and the rest of Palestine then remained in Muslim hands until the early twentieth century, becoming part of the Ottoman Empire in 1517.

Jerusalem fell out of Ottoman control during the First World War. During the autumn and winter of 1917, Allied forces advanced from Egypt through the Sinai into Palestine. Neither they nor the retreating Ottoman and German forces wanted to be held responsible for any damage done to Jerusalem; so when it became clear their position was no longer tenable, the defenders withdrew on the night of 8 December. After the First World War, Jerusalem and the rest of Palestine was ruled by the British as a League of Nations mandate. By this time thousands of Jews had settled in Palestine, inspired by Zionism. This movement to found and establish a Jewish state was a response to the centuries of near-constant scapegoating and persecution, some of it extremely violent. In the Russian Empire, for example, Jews were the focus of pogroms – state-organized campaigns of deadly rioting. There were serious tensions (notably over access to the Temple Mount) between the Arab and Jewish communities, leading to rioting and fighting, as well as skirmishing with the British forces who were unable to prevent the escalating violence.

STADTCASINO BASEL

The man who transformed Zionism into a global campaign was Theodor Herzl (1860– 1904). Born in Budapest, he convened the First Zionist Congress on 29–31 August 1897. It was held in the Swiss city of Basel in the concert hall of its casino. At the meeting, a manifesto setting out Zionism's main goals was agreed. Zionism grew in strength, and Jewish people began to resettle in Palestine. Just half a century after the First Zionist Congress, the State of Israel was founded.

With the British Mandate expiring in 1947, the United Nations promulgated a partition plan for Palestine that recommended Jerusalem be governed as an international city. It was never enacted. In 1948, the State of Israel was proclaimed, and war broke out with its Arab neighbours. Hostilities ended the next year, with the armistice agreement establishing Israel's borders and giving Jordan control of East Jerusalem, which included the Temple Mount. This remained the situation until 1967, when Israeli troops captured Jerusalem during the Six-Day War, prompting great celebration. However, the religious structures of the Temple Mount remained in the hands of a Jordanian 'waqf' (an Islamic charitable endowment) that controls access. Jewish people could visit, but they were not allowed to pray there. Rather, they were permitted to gather and perform religious ceremonies at the Western Wall, the remains of a large retaining wall built by Herod that runs along one side of the Temple Mount. Despite this, the Temple Mount remains a source of tension, and a flashpoint for clashes between Palestinians and Israelis.

THE APADANA AT PARSA

At its height, the Achaemenid dynasty, named after their mythical founder, Achaemenes, ruled a vast, multinational empire that was the largest the world had ever seen at the time. Their ceremonial capital was Parsa, or, as the Ancient Greeks called it, Persepolis.

By 1000 BC, Indo-European tribes had spread out from Central Asia towards the Middle East (as well as settling in Europe, Anatolia and India); they included the Medes and the Persians, related groups that had migrated to modern-day Iran. By this time, the Assyrians had replaced the Babylonians as the dominant power in the region. The Assyrian Empire fell in 612 BC after a series of civil wars and revolts, and it was supplanted by the resurgent Babylonians. In around 558 BC, Cyrus II (*c.* 600–530 BC) succeeded his father as King of Persia, but initially he had to recognize the Medians as his overlords. He rebelled against them and by 548 BC had won control of all Iran, before embarking on a series of campaigns that ranged from Anatolia to Afghanistan. He defeated the Babylonians in 539 BC and proclaimed himself 'king of Babylon, king of Sumer and Akkad, king of the four corners of the world'. Cyrus the Great died in battle in 530 BC fighting nomadic raiders on his northern frontier and was succeeded by his son Cambyses II (d. 522 BC), who conquered Egypt in 525 BC. Under Cambyses's son-in-law Darius I (550–486 BC), who ascended the throne in 521 BC, the empire reached its peak, extending over 3,000 km (2,000 miles) from the western coast of the Black Sea to the Indus River. This vast area was divided into administrative districts called satrapies, which were governed by an official called a satrap who oversaw taxation, public order and judicial affairs. Darius I, whose feats also earned him the appellation 'the Great', balanced centralizing the empire (notably through improving roads and standardizing currency and measurements) with respecting local customs and encouraging religious and cultural tolerance. Darius's imperialist ambitions in Anatolia brought him into conflict with Greek city-states, which had several colonies there. To prevent any interference, in 492 BC, Darius I invaded Greece but was forced to withdraw after defeat at the Battle of Marathon in 490 BC. The second (far larger) Persian attempt to subjugate the Greeks, ten years later, was also thwarted.

THERMOPYLAE

In 480 BC, Xerxes I invaded Greece with perhaps 250,000 men. The Greeks made a stand at Thermopylae, a mountain pass. The 7,000 Greeks at Thermopylae held out for one week before being defeated. Although the Persians then advanced south, the sacrifice at Thermopylae allowed the Greeks to regroup. One month later an Athenian-led navy devastated the Persian fleet at the Battle of Salamis. Xerxes retreated to Asia with the majority of his army, and the next year the Greeks defeated the remaining Persian forces.

The Achaemenid rulers had several capitals, including Babylon, Susa, Pasargadae (which had been established by Cyrus II in 545 BC) and Ecbatana, their summer residence. The city that was the spiritual centre of the dynasty was Parsa. Located in southern Iran, it was fairly remote from the other capitals, where most of the administration was housed. Parsa was a complex of monuments and royal residences that represented the scale and majesty of the Achaemenid Empire. The first stage of the work at Parsa took place between around 520 and 480 BC under Darius I and his son and successor, Xerxes I (519–465 BC). After a hiatus of about thirteen years, Xerxes resumed the work, which was finished by *his* son and successor, Artaxerxes I (d. 424 BC), by around 450 BC. Parsa was built on the spur of a mountain, atop a rock terrace that rose up to 12 metres (40 feet) above the surrounding plains. The platform was reached by a monumental double stairway whose steps were so large that horses could be ridden up them. At the top of the stairs was the 'Gate of All Lands'; through its 12-metre-high (40 feet) wooden doors there were several buildings, all of which were made of blocks of stone cut from the neighbouring mountain, including a throne hall, treasury room, council hall, harem and royal palaces.

The most impressive building in Parsa was the Apadana, which was an audience hall of 3,660 square metres (39,396 square feet), with a roof supported by six rows of six 21-metre-high (70 feet) columns, which were topped by twin-headed bulls, lions or eagles. On the staircases that led up to the Apadana were stone carvings of noblemen, officials and royal guards on the march, as well as depictions of representatives from twenty-three of the far-flung subject nations of the empire, from as far afield as Ethiopia and India, wearing local costume and bringing goods as tribute. On the Persian New Year's Day (the vernal equinox), there was a such a procession of offerings, although it is unknown if delegates actually travelled to Parsa or if it was a ceremonial event carried out by soldiers from those lands who were serving in the multinational imperial army. The Apadana could hold up to 10,000 people, although the ranks of columns and a lack of natural light made it hard to view the king – possibly, this could have been a deliberate decision to preserve his remoteness. Indeed, throughout Parsa the Achaemenid kings are portrayed as semi-divine heroes, the personification of the state, and focus of the offerings and loyalty of their subjects.

In 330 BC, the Achaemenid Empire, which had slowly declined in power, finally fell to Alexander the Great's (356– 323 BC) invading army. That year, having captured Babylon and Susa, he marched on Parsa. Although the city peacefully surrendered to him, Alexander allowed his men to plunder it. They marched out with 120,000 talents worth of gold, silver and other treasure; the loot weighed over 1.2 million kilograms and required 10,000 mules and 500 camels to transport it. Alexander then burned Parsa as punishment for the destruction the Achaemenids had meted out when they had invaded Greece 150 years earlier. Ironically, the mass of burned debris and dust helped to preserve the ruins for archaeologists (formal excavations began in 1878) because it deterred people from carrying away the stones to use as building material elsewhere.

Parsa at first retained some status as a provincial capital but then went into decline under the Seleucid Empire (the dynasty founded by one of Alexander's generals that ruled most of the former territories of the Achaemenids until 63 BC), dwindling away to become a shadow of what it had once been.

THE ACROPOLIS OF ATHENS

. . . .

Few places have matched the long-term historical influence of Athens, which came to symbolize the apex of Ancient Greek culture. Overlooking the city, from its foundation up to the present day, is the Acropolis.

From around 2200 BC, Indo-European peoples migrated to Greece, establishing tribal monarchies and building fortified settlements, the most important of them Mycenae, after which their civilization is named. From 1250 to 1100 BC, Mycenaean Greece collapsed as a result of foreign invasion, internal warfare and natural disasters. It took until 800 BC for Greece to stabilize, when city-states known as *poleis* (plural of *polis*) began to emerge, the most famous of which was Athens.

Athens had been a centre of Mycenaean civilization, and from the thirteenth century BC it was the site of an acropolis ('highest city' in Greek), a walled palace complex built on high ground (nothing of which survives save for a column base and some steps). The Acropolis of Athens occupied seven acres at the summit of a hill 70 m (230 feet) high and would become the nucleus of the city that grew up around it. During the seventh century BC, Athens grew in power and prosperity, gaining control of its neighbouring region, Attica. In 594 BC, to prevent tensions between rich and poor escalating into civil war, Athens adopted a democratic constitution that gave all free men a say in government (although the system gave more powers to wealthier citizens). As Athens grew, new city walls were constructed around its outskirts, so the Acropolis no longer had as much of a defensive function. It became more of a ceremonial site devoted to Athena, the patron of Athens, and during the sixth century BC a monumental temple dedicated to her was built there.

The Acropolis became sacred ground; neither births nor deaths were permitted to take place there, and people who had recently had sexual intercourse had to undergo a purification ceremony before they entered the site. Dogs and goats were not allowed anywhere near the area because they might soil the ground. Stored on the Acropolis was a statue of Athena so old the Athenians did not know its true origins; some believed it came from the heavens, while others thought it was made by a legendary king of the city. Made of olive wood, it was a life-sized woman that every four years was attired in a new woollen robe dyed with saffron made by maiden priestesses. The statue itself was destroyed or crumbled away with age in the early fifth century AD.

Athens and other Greek city-states were active outside their borders, trading and establishing colonies across the Mediterranean. In Anatolia this put them at odds with the

Persian Empire, which in 490 BC invaded Greece. In response, Athens entered an alliance with other *poleis*, the most important of which was Sparta, which repulsed the Persians. That year, the old temple of Athena on the Acropolis was torn down and work began on a new one. When war restarted with Persia in 480 BC it was still unfinished. The Persians soon sacked Athens, laying waste to the Acropolis; burning its buildings, destroying sacred objects and taking away precious metals to melt down (the wooden statue of Athena had been smuggled out beforehand). The next year, the leaders of Athens swore an oath before the Battle of Plataea vowing they would not rebuild the Acropolis until the Persians were defeated. Although the allied Greeks then won a great victory that forced the Persians to retreat, the Athenians wanted to continue the war to ensure they would not meddle in their affairs. This put them at odds with allies, such as Sparta, who desired peace. Athens formed an alliance of like-minded *poleis* called the Delian League, which fought on against Persia. Another conflict began in 460 BC, when tensions between the former Greek allies led to war between the Delian League and the Spartan-led Peloponnesian League. After decades of fighting Athens made peace with Persia in 449 BC and with the Peloponnesian League in 445 BC. By this time, rebuilding work on the Acropolis had begun in earnest. It was part of a city-wide programme overseen by Pericles (*c.* 495–429 BC), the statesman who had led Athens since 461 BC. Foremost among the new buildings on the Acropolis was the Parthenon, which was fully completed in 432 BC and was distinguished by its peristyle of forty-six columns. It replaced the destroyed temple of Athena, as well as acting as the treasury for the Delian League and storehouse of Athens's most valuable ritual objects. Pericles also commissioned the Propylaea, a monumental gateway that controlled access to the Acropolis.

THE PLATONIC ACADEMY

Perhaps Athens's greatest long-term impact came from its philosophers; one of the reasons they were so influential was that they established academies. The most important one was founded by Plato (428/7–348/7 BC), a follower of Socrates (c. 470–399 BC). In 388 BC, Plato founded a school in a sacred grove just outside Athens. It operated until it was destroyed in 86 BC when a Roman army sacked Athens.

War with the Peloponnesian League restarted in 431 BC. Sparta invaded Attica, forcing the Athenians to shelter behind their walls while the surrounding countryside was ravaged. Pericles was criticized for not engaging the enemy, and in 429 BC he died as a result of a plague that killed around half of the city. Despite this, the Spartans and their allies were unable to breach Athens's walls. Throughout pestilence and war, work continued on the Acropolis. In 420 BC, the Temple of Athena Nike, a shrine honouring her in her guise as goddess of victory, was completed. The last of the temples on the Acropolis was the Erechtheum, which was dedicated to Athena and Poseidon and completed in 406 BC. Athens was defeated two years later, leaving Sparta as the dominant force in Greece.

Athens never recovered the influence it had enjoyed in the fifth century BC. During the mid-fourth century BC, it fell under the hegemony of Macedon, which replaced Sparta as the leading force in Greece. The next power to dominate Athens was Rome, which conquered Greece in 146 BC. Roman influence was felt on the Acropolis; in around 19 BC, a small circular shrine dedicated to Rome and Emperor Augustus (63 BC – AD 14) was built in front of the Parthenon. After the Ottoman Empire conquered Greece in the mid-fifteenth century, the Acropolis housed a Turkish garrison, while the Parthenon, which had been serving as a church, was converted into a mosque and later into a gunpowder magazine. This caused serious damage to the Acropolis in 1687, when Venice was besieging Athens and one of its cannonballs struck the building, igniting a huge explosion.

Following years of warfare with the Ottoman Empire, Greek independence was formally recognized in 1832. Athens became its capital, while the Acropolis was cleared of all Turkish artefacts and over the decades has been restored as a symbol of national pride in the golden age of Hellenic civilization.

THE HOUSE OF CONFUCIUS

During the sixth and fifth century BC, China was beset by internal conflict, with local rulers challenging royal authority and battling for dominance. These troubled times forced scholars to consider how to establish order; the most famous of these men was Kongfuzi (551–479 BC), which means 'Master Kong', better known in the West as Confucius, who would become one of the most influential philosophers in world history.

Confucius was born in the state of Lu, which was in modern-day north-eastern China, just outside the capital city, Qufu. His background was not particularly distinguished – his family were minor gentry (known as *shi*), just above the rank of commoners. As a young man, Confucius joined the administration of the local ruler, the Duke of Lu, starting as a low-level bureaucrat and working his way up to be the police commissioner. Although a highly learned and morally upright man, he struggled to gain influence over the Duke, who ignored Confucius's suggestions for reform. Frustrated, in his mid-fifties Confucius resigned his post, left his family home in Qufu, and went in search of a ruler who would listen to his advice. He spent over twelve years travelling across China but was still unable to find a senior position or influence. Therefore, in around 484 BC, Confucius returned home to Lu, where he would win fame, not as a politician, but as a teacher and philosopher.

Back in Qufu, Confucius, who had gained several followers on his sojourn, established a school at his home where he taught students, aiming to train a new generation of more virtuous political leaders and citizens. He was willing to teach anyone, regardless of social rank, and welcomed both rich and poor as students. Instead of forcing them to learn facts by rote, he instructed them through discussion and debate, and was most concerned that his students exhibit high moral behaviour and practise good and responsible government. Confucius instructed his students to learn to appreciate poetry and music, as knowledge of these arts was the mark of a cultivated person. He also placed a great emphasis on teaching history, so people could model themselves on the example of great figures from the past, and apply their wisdom to the present. Confucius died in 479 BC; by this time, he had hundreds of followers from across China (many of whom founded their own schools). During his final illness, he gently reprimanded his students for attending him as if he were a great lord, reminding them that he only wanted a simple funeral.

After Confucius died, his modest three-room house in Qufu would become the foundation of an extensive temple complex, which was made a UNESCO World Heritage Site in 1994. Over the centuries it grew to contain several buildings and hundreds of rooms. The site, which is richly decorated with carvings and sculptures, was often visited by emperors who wished to honour the memory of Confucius. In the seventh century AD, the house where Confucius had lived was moved to an adjacent location. His descendants continued to live in the house, which was redeveloped into an extensive residence with dozens of buildings (152 of which remain). It now covers 7 hectares and houses an extensive collection of historical artefacts and documents. Confucius's tomb, adjacent to his house, is now part of a cemetery that also contains the graves of thousands of his descendants. There are also trees all around the cemetery; many of them date back to ancient times, as after Confucius died, his students kept vigil at his tomb and brought trees from their homes to plant there.

With their mentor gone, some of Confucius's former students assembled his wisdom and sayings (along with teachings from his leading disciples) into a book known as the *Lunyu* (*Analects*), one of the most important works of philosophy in world history. Confucianism was ultimately practical, and focused on how to order personal relationships and society in general. He believed this could be achieved through government by *junzi* ('superior individuals') who were educated and upright. People, he believed, were able to be taught to act with benevolence and kindness, and have deference to their superiors and respect for their parents.

THE MAUSOLEUM OF QIN SHI HUANG

The man who unified the warring Chinese kingdoms was Zheng (259–210 BC), prince of Qin. In 221 BC, having defeated the other six states, he declared himself Emperor of China and took the regal name Qin Shi Huang ('First Emperor of Qin'). Qin established a centralized bureaucratic regime, standardizing laws, introducing a new common script and encouraging the use of coinage. One of his greatest legacies was linking together the various defensive walls that had been built to keep out invading tribes from the north, creating the foundation of the Great Wall of China. Very little of Qin's wall remains – most of the current fortification dates from the Ming dynasty (1368–1644). Qin died of mercury poisoning, having ingested some hoping it would help him live forever. He was buried in a vast underground tomb near the modern city of Xi'an, interred with thousands of life-sized armed soldiers made of terracotta, as well as models of horses, chariots, bureaucrats, servants and entertainers. Qin remained undisturbed until 1974, when workers digging a well found fragments of terracotta, leading to archaeological excavations that uncovered the mausoleum.

This would create an example that others could follow. During the second and first century BC, Confucianism grew increasingly prominent, as its tenets were embraced by the Chinese imperial government as a guiding political and social philosophy. Even centuries after the death of Confucius, his philosophies continued to be important, remaining highly influential, not just in China, but also in Korea, Japan and Vietnam.

THE BODHI TREE IN BODH GAYA

Siddhārtha Gautama inspired Buddhism, which grew to become one of the largest religions in the world. He rose to prominence through preaching across northern India sometime between the sixth and fourth century BC, after achieving spiritual enlightenment while meditating under a bodhi tree.

Siddhārtha Gautama was born in the north-eastern part of the Indian subcontinent, possibly in Lumbini in modern-day Nepal. He came from a wealthy princely Hindu family; his mother died one week after his birth and his father tried to shield him from the harshness of the outside world. Siddhārtha spent the first twenty-nine years of his life living inside a walled palace complex, and at sixteen married a princess called Yaśodharā (some sources suggest they had a son, Rāhula). Siddhārtha's life was transformed when he began to venture forth from his palace. He saw an old man, a sick man and a corpse, which made him realize the suffering that was intrinsic to human existence. Siddhārtha had also seen a mendicant; inspired by his example, he renounced his life of luxury and set out with five other mendicants. They wandered through the countryside and lived a life of extreme asceticism, so that Siddhārtha grew emaciated.

After six years, Siddhārtha sat down under a bodhi tree (a species known as *Ficus religiosa*, and distinguished by its heart-shaped leaves) on the banks of the Lilajan River (located in north-eastern India, in the modern state of Bihar). He had an insight that his lifestyle would not help him find spiritual fulfilment, and he accepted a bowl of milk-rice from a local village-girl called Sujata, leading his compatriots to leave him. Now alone, Siddhārtha ate and resolved to remain under the tree until he had reached enlightenment. A wicked being called Mara, the god of desire, attacked and tempted him in an effort to stop his meditation, but it was not able to. Siddhārtha, after days of consideration, finally experienced enlightenment. He came to understand that humans could attain nirvana, which would allow them to break out of the karmic cycle of death and rebirth, and so became the Buddha ('Awakened One').

The Buddha remained under the tree for seven weeks, reflecting on his experiences. He then rejoined his five former colleagues, and he gave his first sermon to them at the Deer Park in Sarnath, near the city of Varanasi. They became his first five disciples. At the heart of Buddha's teachings was the Four Noble Truths; that there is suffering, that it has a cause, that it can be removed, and that the way to do this is the Eightfold Path (right view, right intention, right speech, right action, right livelihood, right effort, right mindfulness and right meditation). The Buddha then resumed his travels, which were mostly across the Ganges Plain, spending over four decades preaching his message and gathering followers. With the Buddha's advice, they formed into sanghas (communities of monks), which played a vital role in spreading the religion in its early days. Unlike many other religions, women were allowed to join sanghas (and it was also possible for them to achieve nirvana). Siddhārtha also spoke across caste lines – his message was open to all. The Buddha died at around eighty, passing into nirvana.

The figure most responsible for transforming Buddhism into a world religion was Emperor Ashoka (d. *c.* 232 BC), ruler of the Maurya Empire, whose territory would eventually cover most of the Indian subcontinent. Ashoka was not born a Buddhist, and in fact his early life had been characterized by violence and bloodshed. He came to the throne in *c.* 268 BC after a four-year succession conflict, in which he was said to have killed ninety-nine of his brothers, sparing only one. In *c.* 262 BC, he embarked on a successful campaign against the rival kingdom of Kalinga in eastern coastal India; it was so bloody that Ashoka experienced a spiritual awakening and converted to Buddhism. At first he was not always zealous in following his new religion – many of his 'rock edicts', a series of over thirty inscriptions spread across his empire, detail his initial personal struggles to live according to the teachings of Buddha. Ashoka fully supported the religion, trying to build unity among the various sanghas, building thousands of monasteries and stupas (commemorative structures containing relics), and sponsoring missionaries who ranged as far as Sri Lanka and Myanmar. Despite his conversion, Ashoka never forced Buddhism on his subjects – there was freedom of religion across his empire; all he asked was that they live peaceful and moral lives. After Ashoka died, the Maurya Empire fragmented under foreign attacks and civil war, and it collapsed in 185 BC.

The site of the Buddha's enlightenment, and the bodhi tree itself, quickly became a shrine and site of pilgrimage. During the third century BC, Emperor Ashoka built the Mahabodhi Temple around it. Next to the bodhi tree, he built a platform called the Vajrasana ('Diamond Throne') that is said to be on the exact spot where the Buddha meditated. The oldest parts of the present temple complex, which was made a UNESCO World Heritage Site in 2002, date back to the fifth century AD. Since the fourteenth century it has also become a place of pilgrimage for Hindus, and there has been controversy between them and Buddhists about access to the site. Over the centuries the bodhi tree was cut down several times, but on each occasion it miraculously grew back. A bodhi tree still stands at the Mahabodhi Temple, and it may be a descendant of the original specimen the Buddha meditated under. The seeds and cuttings of its branches are used to make prayer beads, which are highly valued. In addition, saplings from the tree were taken and planted in other places. One went as far afield as Sri Lanka, where Ashoka's daughter gave it to the king there. It was planted in Anuradhapura in 288 BC. The tree, known as the Jaya Sri Maha Bodhi, is believed to be the oldest living tree planted by a human, and is a sacred relic.

The canon of Buddha's teachings, known as the *Tripitaka*, was collected after his death and not written until at least two centuries later. In addition, councils were held to define his teachings and answer doctrinal questions. Over the generations, as the religion grew, it split apart several times, with different branches founded across Asia. It was also a major influence on other faiths, such as Confucianism and Shintoism.

THE LIBRARY OF ALEXANDRIA

Alexandria was one of the greatest cities in the ancient world, and an unparalleled centre of learning. Central to its intellectual life was its great library, founded with the lofty ambition of bringing together all of the written works in the world.

THE HYDASPES AND HYPHASIS RIVERS

In 326 BC, Alexander advanced into the Punjab, which was ruled by the warrior-king Porus. They met in battle on the Hydaspes River (now the Jhelum). Alexander won the day; he wanted to conquer the rest of northern India but his Macedonian veterans would only go as far as the Hyphasis River (now the Beas) before they refused to march further. Though undefeated in battle, he had reached the limit of his conquests.

In 336 BC, Philip II of Macedon (382–336 BC), who had transformed his small kingdom into the greatest power in Greece, was assassinated. His successor was his son Alexander (356–323 BC), who solidified his control of Greece before turning his attention to the Achaemenid Persian Empire, which controlled much of Central Asia, the Middle East and North Africa. Alexander led his army across the Dardanelles in 334 BC, conquering Anatolia and Syria. His next target was Egypt, where the local population, unhappy under Achaemenid rule, welcomed him as a liberator when he arrived in 332 BC. The local governor peacefully surrendered to Alexander, who was crowned as Pharaoh. Wintering in Egypt, he was sailing on the Nile Delta and came across a site ideal for a city. The settlement was the first of over twenty that he established, and bore his name:

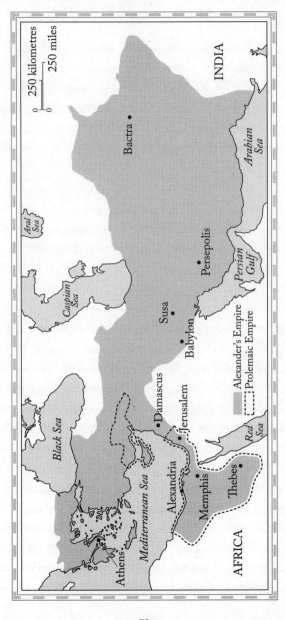

The empire of Alexander the Great, 323 BC

Alexandria. Alexander took a great interest in his foundation, setting out where the agora, temples and walls should be, with the assistance of his advisor the architect Deinocrates of Rhodes.

Alexandria was ideally located; it was on a long natural bay on the western branch of the Nile Delta, giving it excellent connections to the Mediterranean and the rest of the Egypt. Alexander was not the first person to appreciate the usefulness of the site; it had previously housed an Egyptian settlement called Rhacotis. In 331 BC Alexander left Egypt. He invaded Mesopotamia and over the next four years inflicted a series of defeats on the Achaemenids that led to their overthrow, leaving him in control of their empire. He had left Egypt in the hands of local administrators, although dozens of Greek officials kept a close eye on them. Alexandria, which was laid out on a grid, began to take shape. It was mostly settled by Greeks, but there were also Egyptian and Jewish residents.

Alexander, known to history as 'the Great', died in 323 BC in Babylon. He had been unable to establish firm succession plans, and his empire fragmented into civil war between his generals. One of them, Ptolemy (*c.* 367–282 BC), a close friend of Alexander's, took control of Egypt, eventually naming himself its king. He made Alexandria his capital, and his descendants would rule Egypt from there for nearly three centuries. Ptolemy added to Alexandria's prestige by making it the site of Alexander's tomb; his forces had intercepted the funeral cortege as it was travelling back to Macedon. Ptolemy's greatest plan for the city was to build a *Mouseion* for the worship of the Muses, the nine goddesses who inspired creativity and study in the arts, literature and science. It would host not just a temple but a garden, zoo and observatory. Its most famous feature was its library. Ptolemy died in 282 BC and was succeeded by his son Ptolemy II (308/9–246 BC), who oversaw the completion of the *Mouseion* and library. He also finished the construction of the great Lighthouse of Alexandria, which was built on the offshore island of Pharos and stood over 350 feet (106 m) tall.

ANTONY AND CLEOPATRA

Caesar was assassinated in 44 BC. Cleopatra remained ruler of Egypt, becoming involved with Mark Antony (83–30 BC), one of Caesar's chief lieutenants, who she married. In 32 BC, Egypt was plunged into a civil war between Mark Antony and Octavian (63 BC – AD 14), Caesar's grand-nephew and heir. Octavian's forces invaded Egypt and forced Mark Antony to commit suicide in 30 BC. Octavian then entered and occupied Alexandria, where Cleopatra had remained during the fighting. Cleopatra was kept alive but when she heard rumours she was to be taken to Rome to be paraded as Octavian's captive she committed suicide to escape this fate. Octavian, taking the name Augustus, became the first Roman Emperor in 27 BC.

The *Mouseion* was lavishly funded by the wealthy Ptolemaic kings, who were eager to support intellectual pursuits. It hosted a community of around forty learned men, who were given room and board, and exemption from taxation, and were paid a salary to study their subjects, as well as give public lectures and teach. Protection and funding by the Crown meant that scholars in Alexandria enjoyed a high degree of academic freedom. Alexandria lagged behind other Greek cities in poetry and literature, but was foremost in the study of the sciences, particularly medicine, mathematics, mechanics and astronomy. Archimedes of Syracuse (*c.* 287–212 BC), one of the great scientists of antiquity, may have worked in the library, as did the mathematician Euclid (*fl. c.* 300 BC) and the astronomer Aristarchus of Samos (*c.* 310 – *c.* 230 BC), who proposed a heliocentric solar system 1,800 years before the Polish Nicolaus Copernicus (1473–1543) did. The library was overseen by a Crown-appointed official and gathered texts from the Hellenic, Egyptian and Mesopotamian worlds. The Ptolemaic kings were so eager to ensure the completeness of their library that all ships that docked in Alexandria had their cargo inspected for works that were not yet part of the collection, which would be seized and copied. Other works were purchased by Crown agents in cities like Athens and Rhodes. Money was no object. When Ptolemy III (*c.* 280–222 BC) wrote to other states asking for their books for copying, Athens sent several important texts; the library kept the originals, even though it meant the king forfeited his bond of 15 talents (amounting to about 150 kilograms of silver). By the mid-third century BC, there were around 490,000 rolls in the library; over four-fifths of them contained the text of more than one work on them (in addition, over 40,000 works were held in the Serapeum, a temple devoted to the cult of Serapis, a Graeco-Egyptian deity who was patron of Alexandria).

HYPATIA OF ALEXANDRIA

One of the last known members of the *Mouseion* was Theon (c. 335–405), who specialized in mathematics and astronomy. His daughter Hypatia (c. 350–415) was the greatest astronomer and mathematician of her day as well as teaching students in her philosophical school. A pagan, she became the target of hatred, and in 415 she was set upon by a mob of Christian zealots and brutally murdered. The tragic death of Hypatia was symptomatic of Alexandria's decline from being the world's greatest centre of learning.

By the later second century BC, the library had lost much of its prestige, focusing more on overseeing its collection and becoming less of a place of innovation. Mirroring this, the Ptolemaic dynasty declined in power, with the Roman Republic enjoying growing influence over it. When a war of succession between Ptolemy XIII (*c.* 62–47 BC) and his sister

Cleopatra VII (69–30 BC) started in 48 BC, Rome intervened in the shape of Gaius Julius Caesar (100–44 BC). He was in the midst of his own civil war with republican rivals who believed he had grown too powerful. He arrived in Egypt in pursuit of Pompey (106–48 BC), an erstwhile friend who had become his main rival. Pompey had tried to seek refuge with Ptolemy XIII, but he had his guest murdered, believing it would please Caesar and ensure his backing. It did the opposite; Caesar was heartbroken at the death of his former ally. Cleopatra was more successful in her appeals to Caesar; after meeting, the two became lovers. At the Siege of Alexandria, Ptolemy XIII's forces were defeated by Caesar, securing the throne for Cleopatra. This came at a cost for the library. Caesar's soldiers had started a fire in the wharves to block enemy shipping, but the flames accidentally spread to the library, leading to its partial destruction and the loss of over 40,000 rolls. It was rebuilt, and Caesar replenished its collection by gifting Cleopatra 200,000 works from Pergamum, a city in Anatolia that had its own library.

Under Augustus, Egypt became a province of the Roman Empire, while Alexandria remained a wealthy trading city. The library's decline was steady. In 215, Emperor Caracalla (188–217) brutally sacked Alexandria as an act of revenge for perceived criticism from its citizens, causing huge damage to the library. During the 390s, Emperor Theodosius I (347–95), who had declared Christianity the state religion of the Roman Empire, declared a campaign of burning 'pagan' works, which led to the destruction of much of the library's collection. By the time Alexandria was conquered by the Arab Empire in 642, the library was a pale shadow of its former glory, with little or none of its collection left. The ancient institution and its spirit of learning is commemorated by a new modern library and museum complex, the Bibliotheca Alexandrina, which was established in 2002.

THE PANTHEON OF ROME

The Roman Empire reached its greatest size in AD 117, during the reign of Trajan (53–117). His successor, Hadrian (76–138), oversaw the rebuilding of the Pantheon, one of the greatest surviving examples of Roman architectural sophistication.

According to legend, Rome was founded in 753 BC by Romulus, who became its first king. Rome was actually established before this date, possibly in the tenth century BC. Kings ruled Rome until 509 BC, when leading citizens rebelled and abolished the monarchy to establish a republican government. The Roman Republic was not strictly democratic; only free male citizens could vote, and the system gave more power to the wealthy. From the fifth to third century BC, Rome became the leading power in Italy. Rome then began a series of conflicts with the Carthaginian Empire, which had grown from a Phoenician trading colony near modern-day Tunis to rule most of North Africa, southern Spain, Corsica, Sardinia and Sicily. The First Punic War (named after *Punicus*, the Latin for Carthaginian, which originated from 'Phoenician') broke out in 264 BC. Rome built up its naval strength to challenge Carthage and by 241 BC had defeated them and captured Sicily. Three years later, Rome annexed Corsica and Sardinia. The Second Punic War began in 218 BC, when the Carthaginian general Hannibal Barca (247–183/1 BC) invaded Italy via the Alps. Although he won several victories, inflicting heavy casualties, he was unable to capture Rome itself. In 202 BC, Hannibal was forced to return home to face a Roman army that had invaded North Africa. He was defeated 129 km (80 miles) south-west of Carthage at the Battle of Zama. This signalled the end of Carthage's power; it lost its Spanish territories and had to pay a huge indemnity. Hannibal was forced into exile and died in Anatolia, committing suicide after a local king moved to give him up to Rome. The Third Punic War (149–146 BC) saw Rome capture and destroy

Carthage, enslaving its population and annexing its remaining territories. Roman victory over the Carthaginians was followed by conquests in Greece, Anatolia and Syria.

During the first century BC, Rome was beset by internal conflict. Gaius Julius Caesar (100–44 BC) rose to prominence by courting the favour of the people, and from 58 to 50 BC led the conquest and annexation of Gaul (modern-day France). The Senate, fearing Caesar would grow too powerful, ordered him to give up his armies. He refused, and in 49 BC, marched into Italy, sparking a civil war that ended with him winning victory by 44 BC. Caesar was awarded sweeping powers, but was stabbed to death in Rome by a group of conservative senators. The assassination did not restore the status quo. Caesar's adopted son and great-nephew Gaius Octavian (63 BC – AD 19) would establish himself as Emperor of Rome in 27 BC, formally ending the Republic. He adopted the name Augustus, and oversaw further expansion into Iberia, North Africa and Central Europe. After Augustus died, the Roman Empire suffered periodic succession disputes and the violent overthrow of emperors (in AD 69, four different people held the office). Even so, Rome's institutions such as its army, administration, legal system, coinage and transport infrastructure meant it retained its strength despite political upheaval.

One of Augustus's closest allies was his son-in-law Marcus Vipsanius Agrippa (64/2–12 BC). As well as being a statesman and soldier, Agrippa oversaw several building projects in Rome. Many of them were located on the Campus Martius ('Field of Mars'), an area of mostly open, swampy ground just outside Rome. Agrippa transformed the Campus Martius into parkland and added two complexes for citizens to cast votes, the Diribitorium and the Saepta Julia (the latter begun by Caesar), as well as the Thermae Agrippae, a huge public bath, and the Basilica of Neptune, built to celebrate his naval victories. Finally, Agrippa built a rectangular temple dedicated to all gods, called the Pantheon, which was completed between 27 and 25 BC. It was filled with statues of deities such as Mars, Venus and Divus Julius (the deified Julius Caesar). Augustus refused to allow an image of himself to be included within the main sanctuary, although a statue of him was installed in the porch. When Agrippa died, he was honoured by being interred in the Mausoleum of Augustus, which lay on the Campus Martius, north of the Pantheon, where he was later joined by the emperor himself.

In *c.* AD 80, Agrippa's Pantheon burned down and a new temple was built on the site, but little is known about its design. By this time, Roman expansionism was slowing down, and after the first century they mostly avoided expansionist wars, and concentrated on maintaining their borders. No one embodied this policy of retrenchment more than Hadrian (76–138), a former soldier born in Spain who became emperor in 117. He spent much of his reign touring the empire, in an attempt to draw together its vast territory. Hadrian was an active builder, overseeing many projects, including his eponymous border wall built to defend Roman Britain. Hadrian began work on the Pantheon around 118, and it was dedicated between 126 and 128. Its main feature was its dome, the largest in the ancient world. It, and much of the rest of the building, was constructed using concrete, which Roman builders had been using since at least the second century BC. Roman mastery of concrete was not be matched until the later eighteenth century. The dome was cast in one piece by filling a wooden frame with concrete to create a perfect hemispheric form. The frame was then removed after the concrete dried. There was a circular opening, or oculus, at the top of the dome that provided the only natural source of light. The floor was slightly convex so it would drain more quickly if any rain fell through the oculus. It was paved with marble, porphyry and coloured granite that was quarried from as far afield as Egypt and Anatolia. Hadrian kept the original inscription on the front pediment of his Pantheon that attributed the building to Agrippa.

ST PETER'S BASILICA

In AD 64, Peter the Apostle was crucified in Rome; named by Jesus as the 'rock' he would build his church upon, he is viewed as the first pope. In the early fourth century, a basilica was built around Peter's tomb and shrine. By the fifteenth century it was aged and decrepit. The foundation stone for a new basilica was laid in 1506; it took until 1626 for it to be completed; filled with priceless artwork, it was the largest church in the world.

Christianity began to gain followers in Rome from the mid-first century. Despite violent persecution, it attracted more and more converts. The man who transformed the religion's status was Constantine I (*c.* 272–337), who in 313 enacted the Edict of Milan, which ended state persecution of Christianity. In 380, Theodosius I (347–95) declared Christianity the state religion of the Roman Empire. This meant that the Pope, also known as the Bishop of Rome, had a huge amount of prestige, and helped support his claim to be the principal authority in the Church. As Rome was becoming Christian, the power of the emperor was fragmenting.

In 609, the Pantheon was converted into a church and renamed Santa Maria Rotonda. This ensured it would not fall into disrepair or be dismantled for construction materials as many other Roman buildings were. Its 'pagan' decorations were removed and Christian frescoes, paintings and sculptures replaced them. There were many other modifications made to the Pantheon, including the addition of chapels, the removal of its gilded bronze roof tiles, interring the bones of martyrs within it, adding a lead covering over the dome, and building a bell tower above the facade of the porch (it was later removed). When the Renaissance emerged in Italy (later spreading across the rest of Europe) during the later fifteenth and sixteenth century, there was a rediscovery of ancient texts, artworks and buildings. Renaissance figures looked with wonder at the classical buildings, and strove to emulate their style – the dome of the Pantheon was an inspiration for many other buildings, such as Florence Cathedral and St Peter's Basilica.

Despite being highly regarded, the Pantheon did not survive wholly unscathed. Pope Urban VIII (1568–1644) removed the portico's bronze ceiling and melted down the metal to make cannons (some of it was also used to make the great canopy over the high altar of St Peter's Basilica). Urban also added twin bell towers to the front of the Pantheon, but they were torn down in the later nineteenth century. By this time, Italy had been reunified into a single kingdom for the first time since the sixth century. Given that the Pantheon stood as the most visible reminder of Rome, and Italy's, link to its glorious past, it was fitting that the first king of the new Kingdom of Italy, Victor Emmanuel II (1820–78), and his son and successor, Umberto I (1844–1900), were both buried there.

THE SACKS OF ROME

During the later fourth and fifth century, the Roman Empire came under attack from Germanic and Hunnish tribes. Rome became a backwater overshadowed by other cities in Italy, such as Ravenna and Milan. Rome was sacked in 410 by the Visigoths, and in 455 by the Vandals. In 476, the Germanic ruler Odoacer (433–93) sacked Rome and established himself as King of Italy. Although the Roman Empire continued in the east as Byzantium, this was the end of the Western Roman Empire.

4

THE EARLY MEDIEVAL WORLD

· · ❧ · ·

THE TURKISH STRAITS

· ·

Separating Europe and Asia, and the Mediterranean and Black Sea, are two narrow straits, the Bosphorus and the Dardanelles, which are connected by the Sea of Marmara. They have been strategically vital for centuries, particularly after the great metropolis of Constantinople, now known as Istanbul, was founded on the Bosphorus.

During the seventh century BC, Greek colonists founded two settlements on the Bosphorus: Byzantion on the European side, and Chalcedon on the Asian. Control of Byzantion was vital for the Greeks during their wars with Persia during the fifth century BC, and it became an important trading city. It fell under Roman rule, and in AD 324 Emperor Constantine the Great selected it as the site of his new imperial capital and residence.

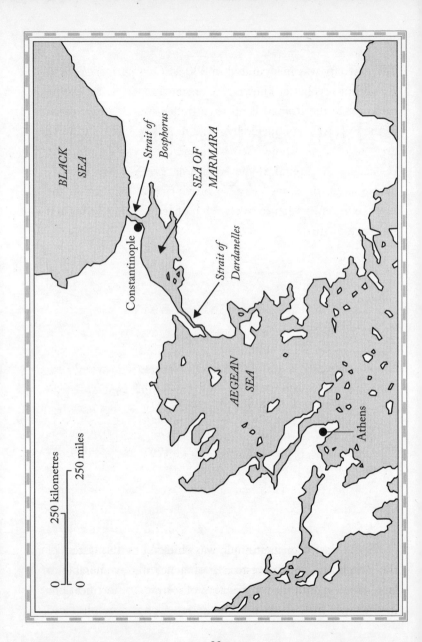

BLACK
SEA

Strait of
Bosphorus

Constantinople

SEA OF
MARMARA

Strait of Dardanelles

AEGEAN
SEA

Athens

250 kilometres

250 miles

0

0

The new city was inaugurated in 330 as *Constantinopolis nova Roma*, but was better known as Constantinople. As the centre of power in the Roman Empire shifted east and its territories in the west were conquered by invading tribes, Constantinople grew to outrank Rome itself in size, wealth and significance. It became the capital of the Byzantine Empire, which was a continuation of Rome's eastern provinces (at its peak in the early sixth century it also ruled much of Italy, North Africa and southern Spain).

THE TROJAN WAR

The Trojan War, which possibly took place in the mid-thirteenth century BC, was the subject of some of Homer's *Odyssey* and *Iliad*, two of the greatest works of Ancient Greek literature. The focus of the conflict was the city of Troy, which may have been located on the Asian side of the Dardanelles. As such, the Trojan War was the first of many conflicts that took place along the Turkish Straits.

To the east, Constantinople was shielded by the waters of the Bosphorus, but its western approaches were vulnerable to land invasion until the construction of formidable fortifications in the early fifth century. Nonetheless, Constantinople faced repeated attacks from foreign powers. In 625, a joint attack by the Avars, a nomadic group from north of the Danube who were advancing from the west by land, and the Persian Empire, invading by sea, was fought off. Two Arab attempts, in 677 and 717–18, were seen off by using Greek fire (a precursor to napalm) against their ships. Likewise, in 941, when the Rus' (who originated from modern-day Russia, Ukraine and Belarus) invaded from the Black Sea, they were repelled using Greek fire. Constantinople was finally conquered in 1204 by a Catholic Crusader army, which led to the dismemberment of the Byzantine Empire. By this time, its power had contracted under pressure from the Seljuq Turks, who had taken most of their territory in the Middle East and Anatolia. The Byzantine emperors reconquered Constantinople in 1261 but their power was on the wane, eclipsed by a new force: the Ottoman Empire.

The Ottomans were a Muslim Turkish people, named after the founder of their dynasty, Osman I (d. 1323/4), who had ruled a small kingdom in Anatolia. After gaining control of all Anatolia, the Ottomans had extended their power across the Turkish Straits to gain territory in Greece and the Balkans. They had been unable to capture Constantinople despite blockading it from 1390 to 1402 and laying siege to it in 1411 and 1422. Under Mehmed II (1432–81) the Ottomans returned for a fourth time, with a mighty force of 160,000, while Constantinople could muster only around 7,000 defenders. Mehmed cut off Constantinople from reinforcements and resupplies before breaching its walls using gunpowder weapons, allowing his men to enter the city. The last Byzantine emperor, Constantine XI Palaiologos (1405–53), was killed in the fighting. Mehmed renamed the city, which became the Ottoman capital, Istanbul; symbolic of the new regime was the transformation of the great Hagia Sophia from a cathedral into a mosque. Over the next 200 years, the Ottoman Empire expanded further into Europe, North Africa and the Middle East.

By the nineteenth century, the Ottoman Empire had greatly shrunk in size and influence, while external enemies and nationalist movements in its provinces threatened to diminish it further. In 1908, the Young Turks, a group of reform-minded officers, seized control of the Ottoman Empire in a revolution and forced the sultan to institute parliamentary constitutional monarchy. They could not prevent defeats in the Italo-Turkish War (1911–12) or the First Balkan War (1912–13), which left the Ottoman Empire denuded of even more territory. To counter the naval power of Greece (which had won full independence from the Ottomans in 1832) and solidify its presence in and around the Turkish Straits, the Ottoman Empire had ordered two modern battleships from the United Kingdom. They had been partly paid for by popular subscription taken across the empire but would never become a part of the Ottoman fleet. On 1 August 1914, a few days after the outbreak of World War I, the two ships were requisitioned by the British government. This led to public outcry in the Ottoman Empire, and forced it closer to Germany. The next day, Germany and the Ottomans signed an alliance, where the Germans would offer military support in return for being allowed movement through Ottoman territory. On 10 August, two German warships arrived at the Dardanelles; they were allowed passage through the Straits and then drafted into the Ottoman Navy. The Ottoman Empire entered the First World War on 29 October, when the two ships attacked Russian ports on the Black Sea. As a result, Russia, the United Kingdom and France all declared war on the Ottomans the next month. Germany provided extensive support for the Ottomans, sending them money, supplies and military personnel. German engineers constructed new batteries on the Dardanelles, along with powerful searchlights to spot enemy ships, undersea nets to deter submarines and a radio-telegraph system to coordinate defences. The waters around the Dardanelles and Bosphorus were even more heavily mined and reinforced.

In February and March 1915, an Anglo-French fleet attacked the Straits, hoping to secure dominance of the route to the Black Sea, which would enable them to resupply Russia more easily. The operation was disastrous for the Allies, with Ottoman artillery and mines wreaking havoc. With the naval operation a failure, the Allies launched an amphibious invasion of the Dardanelles, raising a multinational force of 75,000 with troops from Britain, Newfoundland, New Zealand, Australia, India and France (as well as men from French colonies in Africa). The first landings took place on 25 April, with the Allies establishing two beachheads on the Gallipoli Peninsula (on the European side of the Dardanelles). In Australia and New Zealand, the date is marked as Anzac Day, commemorating the service and sacrifice of soldiers from both countries. The rocky terrain then played host to bitter trench warfare; despite reinforcements arriving in August, the Allies could not permanently advance much beyond their beachheads. By the end of the year, the Allies had begun their retreat from Gallipoli, miraculously managing to make their withdrawal without any fatalities. The last Allied soldiers left on 9 January 1916. In total 142,500 men had died in the campaign (over half of them Turkish).

Ottoman forces carried on fighting in the Balkans, Caucasus and the Middle East while also carrying on a genocidal campaign of killings and deportations against Armenians, Greeks and Assyrians also faced state violence. The Ottomans finally signed an armistice on 30 October 1918, agreeing to allow the Allies access through the Straits. On 13 November, forty-two Allied ships steamed through the Dardanelles to Istanbul, which was then occupied. In 1920, the Ottoman Empire signed the Treaty of Sèvres, which gave its non-Turkish territories independence. Allied troops remained in Istanbul and the Straits were placed under the authority of an international commission that the Ottoman Empire could only join if and when it was admitted to the League of Nations. In response to the terms, the army officer Mustafa Kemal (1881–1938) led an armed nationalist uprising that rejected Sèvres. This Turkish War of Independence resulted in the overthrow of the Ottoman Empire and the declaration of the Republic of Turkey in 1923. Its borders were recognized by the Allies under the Treaty of Lausanne, which also declared that the Straits would be an international zone governed by a commission chaired by a Turk – it was also demilitarized save for a small garrison in Istanbul.

Kemal became president, serving until his death in 1938, and passed a series of modernizing reforms; he was later given the surname Atatürk, meaning 'Father of the Turks'. He oversaw the 1936 Montreux Convention Regarding the Regime of the Straits. This gave Turkey full control of the Straits, allowing it to remilitarize them, while guaranteeing unrestricted travel for all commercial vessels from nations not at war with Turkey. This agreement continues to govern the Turkish Straits, which remain one of the most important sea routes in the world.

THE STRAITS CONVENTION

Although the Ottoman Empire declined during the nineteenth century, it retained control of the strategically vital Turkish Straits. However, in 1833, the Ottomans signed the Treaty of Hünkâr Iskelesi with Russia, agreeing to close the Straits to foreign warships should the Russians request it. The potential for Russia to dominate the route from the Black Sea to the Mediterranean concerned other major powers and led to the 1841 London Straits Convention. This restored Ottoman power by closing the Straits to all foreign military vessels during peacetime and only allowing its allies to use it during war.

CHURCH OF OUR LADY MARY OF ZION

The Kingdom of Aksum, which originated in modern-day Ethiopia, was one of Africa's greatest medieval powers. It was the reputed keeper of the Ark of the Covenant, a relic holy to both Jews and Christians, which was held in the Church of Our Lady Mary of Zion.

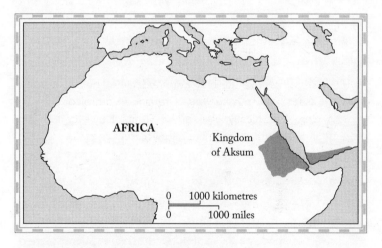

The Kingdom of Aksum, mid-sixth century AD

During the tenth century BC, the semi-mythical Queen of Sheba was said to have travelled to Jerusalem, where she met King Solomon, impressing him with her fabulous gifts and intellect, before converting to Judaism and returning home.

According to Ethiopian sources, she was called Makeda, came from Ethiopia, and had a son with Solomon called Menelik. As a young adult, he travelled back to Jerusalem to meet his father before returning home to rule Ethiopia, establishing a dynasty that lasted for nearly three millennia. It is claimed that he brought with him the Ark of the Covenant, the gold-covered wooden chest that contained the stone tablets that bore the Ten Commandments.

Aksum is in the Tigray highlands of northern Ethiopia. It was the centre of a kingdom that rose to prominence during the second and third century AD. One of the foundations of its growth was commerce; Aksumite merchants established links with the Graeco-Roman world and places as far afield as India, dominating the trading routes that brought goods from the interior of Africa to their ports on the Red Sea. The kings of Aksum, who claimed ancestry from Menelik, adopted Christianity in the second quarter of the fourth century, during the reign of Ezana (d. *c.* 360). He had been educated by a Syrian Christian called Frumentius (d. *c.* 383), a freed slave who had risen to favour at court and been allowed to spread his faith. Frumentius then travelled north to Alexandria to meet the patriarch, who made him a bishop. He returned to Aksum, where he baptized Ezana. Ethiopia thus became the second country to make Christianity its state religion (following Armenia, which had done so in 301). The Ethiopian Orthodox Church retained its own traditions and remained very distinct from Catholicism, particularly as it did not accept papal supremacy. The Ethiopian population was Christianized, as missionaries spread the faith across the land. As Frumentius had established his episcopacy in the city of Aksum, a cathedral, the Church of Our Lady Mary of Zion was built there. It was an 595-square-metre (80-square-foot) building at the centre of a walled complex, and was said to have become the home of the Ark of the Covenant.

By the mid-sixth century, Aksum had extended it borders beyond modern-day Ethiopia and Eritrea, ruling parts of southern Arabia, Sudan, Egypt, Djibouti and Somalia. However, during the seventh and eighth century, the power of the Aksumite kings declined as the Islamic caliphate encroached on their territory, conquering their lands in Arabia and disrupting their trade routes. The city of Aksum became less prosperous, although it remained an important religious centre thanks to the cathedral. In the mid-tenth century, a foreign, possibly Jewish, queen called Gudit attacked Aksum, destroying St Mary of Zion and effectively ending the Kingdom of Aksum. It was not until 1137 that another dynasty, the Zagwe, gained control over Ethiopia, although in 1270 they were overthrown by a prince who claimed descent from the Kings of Aksum (and therefore Solomon and the Queen of Sheba), who established the Ethiopian Empire. St Mary of Zion, which had been rebuilt, became the traditional place of coronation for the Ethiopian emperors.

For Europeans, Ethiopia remained a land of mystery – during the medieval era, some believed it was the home of 'Prester John', a wealthy and powerful Christian king. Even after Portuguese explorers and traders arrived in Ethiopia during the later fifteenth century, many still associated the

Ethiopian emperor with the fabled lost monarch. In 1529, the Ethiopian Empire was invaded by the Adal Sultanate, a Muslim state centred on modern-day Somalia. Its leader, Ahmad ibn Ibrahim (c. 1506–43), occupied and annexed most the country; attacking Aksum and burning St Mary of Zion. It took until 1543 for the Ethiopian emperors to regain control of their lands when, allied with Portugal (seeking to protect their interests in the region), they defeated and killed Ahmad in battle. In 1563, Emperor Sarsa Dengel (1550–97) celebrated his coronation in Aksum and then built a small church in the ruins of St Mary of Zion. It was destroyed in 1611 by the Oromo people, who had invaded from their homeland located in modern-day southern Ethiopia and northern Kenya. The Oromo destabilized the position of the Ethiopian emperors, who were also increasingly influenced by Jesuit missionaries. This culminated in Emperor Susenyos I (1572–1632) declaring Catholicism the state religion in 1622, a highly unpopular decision that placed him at odds with his subjects. Following disorder, in 1632, he was forced to abdicate in favour of his son Fasilides (1603–67), who restored Ethiopian Orthodoxy. He also oversaw the construction of the present St Mary of Zion, which had many Portuguese and Indian influences, and was completed in 1665.

The Ethiopian Empire retained its independence as European states carved up the rest of Africa among themselves during the later nineteenth and early twentieth century. Under the influence of Emperor Haile Selassie I (1892–1975), who came to the throne in 1930 having served as regent for the previous fifteen years, Ethiopia modernized; slavery was abolished, infrastructure was improved, and it became a member of the League of Nations. In 1935, Italy invaded Ethiopia. Armed with tanks, aeroplanes and poison gas, within two years they had defeated Ethiopian forces and annexed the country. Haile Selassie travelled to Geneva to appeal to the League of Nations, but it did nothing to protect the sovereignty of one of its member states. With his country under enemy occupation, Haile Selassie went into exile in England. He returned home in 1941 at the head of an Allied army, when Ethiopia became the first country to be liberated from Axis control. Haile Selassie continued to rule, and in 1965 constructed a new, modern cathedral with a concrete dome at Aksum near the site of the original St Mary of Zion. Haile Selassie was overthrown in 1974 by the Derg, a communist military dictatorship that ruled Ethiopia until 1987. Aksum is now a small district centre, and not even a provincial capital, although the Ethiopian Orthodox Church still claims it is the true home of the Ark of the Covenant.

THE CAVE OF HIRA

Jabal al-Nour is a mountain in western Saudi Arabia on the outskirts of Mecca. On its slopes is the Cave of Hira, where the Prophet Muhammad (*c.* 570–632) received a divine revelation that would inspire him to found a new faith.

Mecca is the home of the Kaaba, a cube-shaped building (supposedly built by Abraham and his son Ishmael) that housed a sacred black stone, which contained pagan idols and was a centre of pilgrimage for the polytheistic inhabitants of the region. By the sixth century, Mecca was ruled by the mercantile Quraysh tribe, who turned it into an important trading hub.

Muhammad, born c. 570, was a member of the Quraysh. Orphaned by the age of six, he was raised by his uncle and worked as merchant. In his mid-twenties, Muhammad married Khadija (555–620), a successful female trader who had hired him to guide a caravan to Syria. As he aged, Muhammad withdrew from Mecca for long periods of solitary reflection in the Sirat Mountains that surround the city. In around 610, Muhammad was meditating in the Cave of Hira, a small natural chamber in the Jabal al-Nour ('Mountain of Light'). He received a visitation from the angel Gabriel in an event known as the 'Night of Power', where the opening verses of the Quran were revealed to him (he would gradually reveal the rest of the holy book to his followers until the year of his death). Initially, Muhammad feared he might have been possessed, but he was reassured by Khadija. Muhammad continued to retreat to the mountains for spiritual reflection, often spending several days in the Cave of Hira. The beliefs that formed the religion of Islam were gradually formed. At first, Muhammad only mentioned his new revelation to close family, but after three years he began preaching in public, gaining followers among the people of Mecca. The wealth of Khadija, who died in 620, was vital in supporting him in the early years of Islam.

As Muhammad preached that there was no god but Allah, he was brought into conflict with the pagan rulers of Mecca. The small group of Muslims faced violence and eventually the situation became so hostile that, in 622, Muhammad and his followers migrated over 480 km (300 miles) north to seek refuge in the city of Medina. There, Muhammad continued to gain converts. In 624, following some raids on their caravans, warfare broke out between the Muslims and Mecca. After six years, Muhammad forced Mecca to agree to peace, before going on to win control of most of Arabia. In 632, Muhammad led the Farewell Pilgrimage to Mecca. It ended at the Kaaba, which, cleared of idols, was ordained as the *qibla* – the direction that Muslims should face when at prayer. This set the tradition of the *Hajj*, the pilgrimage to Mecca that all devout Muslims are expected to make. Muhammad died a few weeks later in Medina.

Muhammad had no surviving sons, and had not clarified who would lead Islam after he died. One of his closest advisors, Abu Bakr (*c.* 573–634), was selected to become the first caliph ('successor'). Over the remainder of the seventh century, the power of the caliphate steadily grew, first extending into Syria and Iraq, before fighting the Byzantine and Sasanian empires to gain territory in Persia, the Caucasus, Anatolia and North Africa. In 661, the Umayyads, a powerful clan from Mecca, won control of the caliphate, instituting hereditary rule and establishing their capital in Damascus, Syria. The division of Islam into its two main branches, Sunni and Shia, can be traced back to this period, and the debate over who should succeed Muhammad. In 656, Muhammad's cousin and son-in-law

Ali (601–61) had become caliph but struggled to impose his authority and was murdered by a political opponent in Kufa in Iraq. He was succeeded by his rival, Muawiyyah (*c.* 602–80), the founder of the Umayyad dynasty. Ali was survived by two sons, Hassan (624–70) and Hussein (626–80), who were allowed to retire peacefully to Medina. Hassan died there in 670, but in 680 opponents of the Umayyads in Kufa invited Hussein to lead a rebellion against them. Hussein rode north to Iraq with his family and supporters but was intercepted by a larger Umayyad force. He refused to surrender, and was executed along with most of his party. The site of Hussein's death became a shrine, and the pilgrims it attracted meant it grew into the city of Karbala. Over the later seventh and eighth century, there were more revolts against the Umayyads by those who believed that only Ali's descendants should lead Islam. This hardened into an ideological split, with the Shi'ites (which originates from the Arabic for 'party of Ali') establishing their own practices and beliefs. Shia now make up over 10 per cent of Muslims worldwide.

Despite, these internal struggles, the caliphate continued to grow. During the eighth century, after conquering most of North Africa, the Umayyads crossed the Strait of Gibraltar and conquered much of the Iberian Peninsula. In 750, the Abbasid family, who were descended from Muhammad's uncle, overthrew the Umayyads to claim control of the caliphate. To rule their empire they established a new capital, called Baghdad, on the site of a small Persian village, which lay on the banks of the Tigris River, north of the ancient metropolis of Babylon.

Around it, Baghdad grew to be one of the largest, wealthiest and most culturally important cities in the world. Abbasid authority steadily dwindled as a result of foreign invasion and internal disorder, culminating in the Mongol Empire invading Mesopotamia and sacking Baghdad in 1258.

THE HOUSE OF WISDOM

At Baghdad's heart was the Madinat al-Salam ('City of Peace'), which housed the Abbasid court and bureaucracy. The Abbasids also founded the House of Wisdom there, a centre of learning that was home to scholars who made important discoveries, spread new ideas from India (such as its numerical system), and preserved classical Greek and Latin texts by translating them into Arabic. In 1258, Baghdad was sacked by the Mongols, but it remained an important city and in 1920 became the capital of the new nation of Iraq.

Despite Mecca's religious significance, political power in the Muslim world resided in other cities, such as Medina, Damascus, Baghdad, Cairo and Istanbul. Mecca, once a thriving commercial hub, relied on the pilgrims who travelled there. By the tenth century, it was ruled by the Sharifs of Mecca, who were Muhammad's direct descendants. They continued in this office after the Ottoman Empire gained control of Arabia in the sixteenth century. During the First World War, the sharif allied with the British to lead the Arab Revolt against the Ottomans. However, his hopes of establishing himself as the ruler of an extensive Arab state in the Middle East were dashed, and in 1925 the House of Saud, who originated from central Arabia, dislodged the sharifs and conquered Mecca. The Sauds became the ruling family of the Kingdom of Saudi Arabia, which was founded in 1932. With the help of revenues from their petroleum reserves, they have invested heavily in Mecca, carrying out extensive building and renovation work. The Cave of Hira remains the same as it was in the Prophet's day, providing a link to the founding moment of Islam.

THINGVELLIR

In Germanic and Nordic societies, freemen often met to settle disputes and make decisions. These meetings (known as *things*) evolved into bodies that became popular assemblies. The oldest such body is the Icelandic Althing, which met on a plain on the southern part of the island and became known as Thingvellir.

The Vikings originated in Scandinavia, and from the later eighth century launched raids on coastal areas of Europe; over the next three centuries, their longships were a sight feared across the continent. They established trading links as far afield as the Middle East and North Africa, and migrated to other lands,

Viking expansion, eighth to tenth century AD

particularly Britain, Ireland and Normandy. Skilled navigators, Vikings discovered new lands and colonized islands in the North Sea and Atlantic Ocean. Their largest colony was Iceland, which remained uninhabited until the late ninth century, although prior to this, small communities of Irish monks and hermits were recorded as settling on the island, and the Greek explorer Pytheas of Massalia may have landed there as early as the fourth century BC. In around 867, the Norseman Ingólfr Arnarson made a voyage to Iceland; he returned in 870 to establish the first Viking settlement there, and was joined by several other families.

The Althing was established in 930; it was the first *thing* whose jurisdiction covered an entire country. Its existence was vital to creating a sense of national unity and helped to prevent regional fragmentation. It enabled a communal, nationwide method of settling disputes, with panels of householders acting as judges (in addition, there were four regional courts). The Althing met every year for two weeks in June on the Thingvellir ('Thing Plain'), one of the few times of the year when there was sufficient daylight and the weather was mild enough for the body to meet. Everything was held in the open air; most people pitched tents or built turf booths, as the only permanent buildings in the vicinity were two churches and a farm. In addition, pedlars and tradesmen operated on the banks of the Öxará ('Axe River'), which ran through the Thingvellir. Although all freemen were permitted to attend, legislative decisions were left to local chieftains (*godard*), who from 965 had their number limited to thirty-nine. They formed the majority of the law council (*lögrétta*), which debated and voted on matters of law as well as making treaties with other nations. Participants sat on benches in three concentric circles, with chieftains sat on the middle one so they could be flanked by their advisors. Under this system, no single person was invested with executive power. The most important and prestigious official was the law-speaker (*lögsögumadr*), who was the elected chairman, on a three-year term, of the law council. He was charged with advising the law council and announcing new legislation passed by them. Every year he had to publicly recite one-third of Iceland's laws from memory at a rocky outcrop called the Lögberg ('Law Rock').

GREENLAND AND VINLAND

During the tenth century, the Vikings ranged beyond Iceland to colonize southern Greenland. In around 1000, Vikings sailed further west and landed in a region they named Vinland. They thus became the first Europeans to make landfall on the American continent. The precise site of their landing is unknown, but it was likely somewhere on the Gulf of Saint Lawrence in modern-day eastern Canada. Subsequent attempts to found Viking colonies in Vinland were abandoned after skirmishes with the indigenous population.

During the later tenth century, the Christian king of Norway began sending missionaries to Iceland. They faced hostility, which led the Norwegian king to threaten to sever trade links with Iceland. When the Althing gathered in 1000, its members debated whether to retain their traditional pagan faith or convert to Christianity. With neither faction willing to submit, it was decided to leave the matter in the hands of the law-speaker Thorgeir Ljosvetningagodi (b. *c.* 940). Although he was a pagan priest, he decided that to secure Iceland's future, it must accept Christianity. His decision was heeded, and Iceland became Christian. During the thirteenth century, Iceland descended into civil war between rival chieftains. In an attempt to find peace, from 1262 Iceland agreed to become subject to Norway. Under the terms of the treaty of union agreed by the Althing, the Icelandic people would become subjects of the Norwegian Crown and pay taxes to it. In 1397, Norway joined with Sweden and Denmark to form the Kalmar Union. Sweden left the union in 1523, leaving Iceland part of Denmark-Norway. In 1662, its king, Frederick III (1609–70), as part of his effort to become an absolute monarch, declared he had sole power to legislate for Iceland. The Althing was not abolished but its influence shrank as it became a court of appeals attended by just a few local farmers. From the 1690s, the Law Council met in a small tent house, before moving to a leaky and draughty timber building in the second half of the eighteenth century. The final session of the Althing at Thingvellir was held in 1798, and it was abolished in 1800. In 1814, the Dano-Norwegian union was broken up, and Denmark was granted possession of Iceland. In 1844, the Althing recommenced at Reykjavik as a consultative body that advised the Danish Crown. After Iceland won limited home rule in 1874, the Althing was given the power to pass legislation on domestic matters. In 1881, it moved into its present home, the Althingishusid. It would take until 1918 for Iceland to win full independence, which meant that the Althing would once more function as the true national parliament. The last time the Althing met at the Thingvellir was on 17 June 1944, when Iceland declared itself a republic.

GREAT ZIMBABWE

By 1000, the Bantu peoples had settled across sub-Saharan Africa, establishing many regional polities. One of the largest and most powerful was the Kingdom of Zimbabwe, whose capital, known as Great Zimbabwe, flourished from the eleventh to fifteenth century.

The Bantu originated in West Africa around 2000 BC, and over the next three millennia they spread out across the continent south of the Sahara. In doing so, they displaced or absorbed hunter-gatherer societies, introducing agriculture and iron-working to the areas they settled. As they migrated over such a vast area, the Bantu developed a diverse range of different cultures and polities.

One of the largest Bantu groups was the Shona, who settled in southern Africa and established the Kingdom of Zimbabwe, which eventually, through conquest, ruled territory that covered around 2,500 square km (1,000 square miles). Zimbabwe is a Shona word that is a contraction of either *dzimba dza mabwe* ('house of stone') or *dzimba woye* ('venerated or respected houses'). The capital of the Kingdom of Zimbabwe is in modern-day south-eastern Zimbabwe, near the city of Masvingo. Known as Great Zimbabwe, it is the largest of around 150 ruins in the same style that exist in the region. It was built in around 1000; it was at first fairly modest and limited in size until the period between 1300 and 1450, when the prosperity and power of the rulers peaked, leading to much new construction that extended the site to around 800,000 square m (200 acres). By this time, the population of Great Zimbabwe and the surrounding settlements may have reached between 10,000 and 20,000.

Great Zimbabwe is divided into three main areas: the Hill Complex, the Great Enclosure and the Valley Ruins that lie between them. The Hill Complex, which is the oldest part of the site, lies on a steep hill and was probably the religious centre of the city. It contains six posts topped with birds, possibly used in rituals, and it was also the burial site of the hereditary rulers of Zimbabwe and may have at first been their residence. The Great Enclosure, built in the fourteenth century, is to the south of this. It is one of the largest surviving pre-colonial structures in sub-Saharan Africa, with an outer wall over 244 m (800 feet) long, made partly of huge granite blocks. The walls were not for defence, as they did not enclose the site or have many military features. Rather, through their massive size they were expressions of the power of the city. One of the main structures in this area is the 10-metre-high (33-foot) 'Conical Tower' – this may have been a symbolic grain bin, showing the largesse of the king to his subjects. Also inside the Great Enclosure were the residences of the king and his immediate relatives. They lived in walled-off areas that contained two brick-built huts and a kitchen area. Finally, there was the Valley Complex, which appears to have emerged as the city grew. It mostly contained residences, housing the king's extended family, officials and other citizens of the city. In addition to housing, manufacturing took place in Great Zimbabwe, with evidence of both pottery and metal-smelting.

KINGDOM OF KONGO

The largest Bantu power was the Kingdom of Kongo, which was founded in around 1390 and grew to rule much of western Central Africa. In 1483, Portugal established commercial and diplomatic relations with Kongo, and traded manufactured goods for copper, ivory and slaves. Over the seventeenth and eighteenth century, Kongo's power declined due to conflict with Portugal and civil war. In 1857, Kongo became a Portuguese vassal, and in 1914 the monarchy was abolished and its remaining territories became part of Portugal's colonial empire.

At first, the mainstay of the Kingdom of Zimbabwe's wealth and power was cattle. Accordingly, the site of Great Zimbabwe was chosen because it was on an interior plateau that had a temperate climate and excellent land for farming and grazing. However, the region around the city was rich in gold, which would become a vital commodity in trade. As such, by the fourteenth century, Zimbabwe was trading goods, particularly gold and ivory, with coastal cities in East Africa. This brought items such as glass beads, salt, cowrie shells and brass wire to the capital. Furthermore, shards of Chinese and Persian pottery have been found there, suggesting it was part of a thriving network of long-distance trade with Asia.

Despite its wealth, by around 1500 Great Zimbabwe had been abandoned, with its inhabitants moving southward. This was probably because the countryside around the city could no longer support its demand for food. The influence of the Kingdom of Zimbabwe rapidly declined, as other powers in the region rose to supplant it. Although Portuguese merchants who arrived in the region during the early sixteenth century were aware of Great Zimbabwe, it was not until the later nineteenth century that European explorers began to visit the ruins. Some of them theorized that it was the site of King Solomon's mythical mines, Queen Sheba's capital, or that it was built by a foreign civilization such as Greece, Egypt or Phoenicia. By the 1890s, the former territory of the Kingdom of Zimbabwe had fallen under British colonial rule, with the area named Southern Rhodesia after the British businessman, politician and imperialist Cecil Rhodes (1853–1902). It declared independence in 1965 as Rhodesia, and the white minority ruled until 1980. The nation was renamed Zimbabwe, after the ancient Shona kingdom that had become an important symbol for the black nationalists who had fought for majority rule. Great Zimbabwe has played a huge role in the identity of the nation; it has been made a national monument, with World Heritage status awarded in 1986, and the soapstone figurines of birds found in the ruins have been incorporated into the national flag, coat of arms and banknotes.

THE UNIVERSITY OF TIMBUKTU

Timbuktu has entered the Western imagination as a byword for remote exoticism, but in reality for centuries it was a thriving centre of learning and commerce, the most important 'port' on the great desert sea of the Sahara.

The Sahara, the largest desert in the world, covers over 7.8 million square km (3 million square miles) of Africa; bordered to the north by the continent's Mediterranean coast and to the south by the semi-arid Sahel region that gives way to tropical savanna. As a result of the Sahara's harsh climate, for much of human history there was little regular contact between West Africa and Eurasia. Crossing such a vast expanse was dangerous, time-consuming and costly, and there was simply not the incentive to do so regularly until the fourth century AD, when people from outside West Africa learned of the region's rich deposits of gold, and caravans began to cross the desert. The trade was dominated by the Berbers, whose camels were the only animals capable of making the journey, which took around three months. As well as gold, Berber merchants purchased slaves, hides, ivory, ostrich feathers, kola nuts and gum. The most crucial commodity the Berbers brought with them was salt, which was in relatively short supply in West Africa, but they also imported horses, cowrie shells, metal goods, spices, perfumes, luxury textiles and dried fruits. Commerce was facilitated by the rise of the Ghana Empire, which brought peace and order to West Africa. During the seventh and eighth century, the Muslim Arabs conquered North Africa, introducing their language and religion. The Berbers converted to Islam, and introduced it to West Africa, where it found many new adherents, particularly in urban areas.

Around 1,100 nomadic Tuaregs, part of the Berber ethnic group, founded a camp on the southern edge of the Sahara. They named it Timbuktu, which means 'mother with a large navel', after the elderly woman who oversaw the camp. It was about 9.5 km (6 miles) north of the Niger River, which runs through West Africa in a great crescent 4,200 km (2,600 miles) long. The river was vital to Timbuktu because it provided a reliable water source as well as a method of transporting goods from and into the rest of West Africa. Crucially, Timbuktu was far enough away from the Niger to avoid being flooded when it overflowed. Over the twelfth and early thirteenth century, Timbuktu expanded into an important market town. From its foundation it was exposed to Islam through contact with North African traders, and histories of the city boast that it was never 'sullied by the worship of idols'.

THE GHANA EMPIRE

The Ghana Empire, founded around 700, grew to cover parts of modern-day Mauritania, Mali and Senegal. Gold was the foundation of the empire's wealth, attracting traders from North Africa who travelled across the Sahara. Over time, the empire fragmented, and by 1240 its remaining territory had been incorporated into the Mali Empire. The legacy of the Ghana Empire remained powerful. When the British colony of the Gold Coast (located hundreds of miles to the south) won independence in 1957, it renamed itself Ghana.

The Mali Empire, whose rulers converted to Islam by the mid-eleventh century, grew from being a minor kingdom to supplant the Ghana Empire as the most important power in West Africa by the early thirteenth century. The most successful *mansa* (which means 'sultan' or 'emperor') of the Mali Empire was Musa I (*c.* 1280 – *c.* 1337), who came to the throne in around 1307. He extended his realms through conquest, winning vast wealth through his control of trade in his territory, and becoming a famed figure in the Muslim world after his 1324–5 pilgrimage to Mecca, on which he was accompanied by 60,000 courtiers and attendants. Musa's generous spending was such that his visit caused the value of gold in Cairo to drop by one-fifth. On his way home, Musa passed through Timbuktu, and the city was added to his empire. It retained a high degree of autonomy and was governed by a group of its leading families, helped by local judges, scholars and imams. This political situation continued after Timbuktu fell, in 1468, to the Songhai Empire, which grew to eclipse Mali as the dominant power in the region. By this time, generations of settlers from across Africa and the Middle East had flocked to Timbuktu, increasing its population to a peak of around 100,000, making it larger than London was at the time. Being part of imperial powers like Mali and Songhai gave Timbuktu status and prestige, as well as delivering peace and security that protected trade.

During the fourteenth and fifteenth century, three mosques were built in Timbuktu: Djinguereber (which was personally commissioned by Musa I), Sankoré and Sidi Yahya. Like the

other buildings in the city, they were mostly constructed using mud bricks, which were made by mixing water with earth. This material was cheap and easy to make, but does require regular reapplication of plaster made from wet soil to maintain the building's appearance and integrity. Craftsmen and architects came from across the Islamic world, including from Yemen and Granada, to build and decorate the mosques. These three mosques acted as places of worship and charitable foundations, but their greatest reputation was as centres of learning, together forming the city's 'university'. As scholars travelled to Timbuktu from as far afield as Egypt and Mecca, it was exposed to ideas from across the Muslim world, and its extensive libraries held hundreds of thousands of books and rare manuscripts. Alongside the *madrassa*s (religious schools) based at the three mosques, there were over 150 smaller educational foundations. In addition to studying Islam, it was possible to receive expert instruction in other fields, including law, philosophy, science and rhetoric. Timbuktu was central to spreading Islam into sub-Saharan Africa, making Islam the dominant religion in many parts of the region.

Starting with Portugal, European powers began to trade directly with West Africa via the Atlantic from the later fifteenth century; as a result, the slower trans-Saharan routes diminished in importance; consequently, Timbuktu declined in size and wealth. In 1591, it was occupied by the forces of the Sultan of Morocco; under their rule many scholars were arrested on suspicion of disloyalty and the city was regularly plundered by raiding tribes, particularly from the Tuareg peoples. Moroccan rule ended in 1620, and Timbuktu returned to self-rule. The 'university' of Timbuktu continued to operate, but the city was a shadow of its former self. In 1894, Timbuktu was annexed by France, and it remained part of the French colonial empire until 1960, when it became part of the independent Republic of Mali. Timbuktu and its libraries were listed as being a UNESCO World Heritage Site in 1988, and there have been great efforts made to preserve its mosques, which had fallen into disrepair. To make matters worse, Timbuktu has been caught up in the civil war between the Malian government and Tuareg and Islamist rebels. When Islamist militants won control of Timbuktu in 2012–13, they destroyed or damaged many of its historic monuments, tombs (the city is said to be the resting place of 333 Muslim saints) and artefacts, believing them to be idolatrous. Efforts to restore Timbuktu to its former glory and preserve its store of precious manuscripts are ongoing, but struggle in the face of poverty and internal disorder.

5

THE LATER MEDIEVAL WORLD

SAMARKAND

Since the second century BC, Europe and Asia have been linked by the Silk Road, a network of trade routes that connected the two continents until the mid-fifteenth century. One of the most important stops en route was Samarkand, which became one of the grandest cities in Central Asia.

The history of Samarkand stretches back as far as the seventh century BC, when it was part of Sogdiana, an ancient Central Asian civilization. It was conquered by the Achaemenid Empire in the mid-sixth century BC, and the Apadana at Parsa shows Sogdians paying tribute to the Persians. Having briefly won its independence in 400 BC, Sogdiana was conquered by Alexander the Great in 329 BC. Drawn into the Hellenic world, Samarkand became a hub of the Silk Road, as from

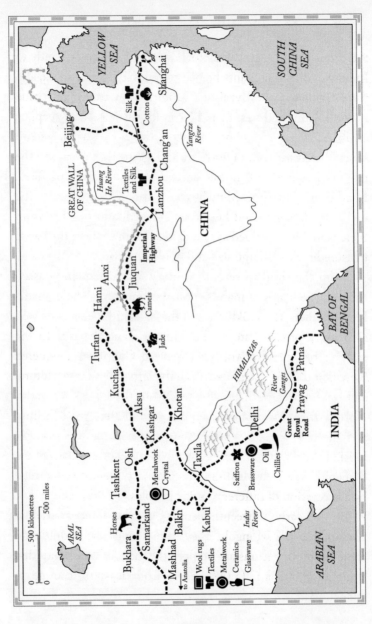

The principal routes of the Silk Road and the goods that were traded, thirteenth to fourteenth century AD

there one could travel west to the Middle East or south to India. Sogdian merchants helped to link China and India, and forged routes to the Byzantine Empire. They traded in a wide range of commodities, including gold, silver, saffron, pepper, camphor, linen and, above all, silk. The Sogdians helped to spread Buddhism out of northern India into East Asia, and the religion was practised in Samarkand (as were Zoroastrianism, Hinduism, Judaism, Manichaeism and Christianity). The orchards of Samarkand became renowned, and peaches from there were highly valued as far afield as China, where they were treasured for their large size and golden colour.

From the third to seventh century AD, Samarkand passed through the hands of many conquerers, including the nomadic Hepththalites, the Göktürks and the Sassanid Persians, as well as being a protectorate of the Chinese Tang dynasty. In the early eighth century AD, the Umayyad Caliphate conquered Samarkand. This integrated the city into a far-flung cultural and economic network that extended to the Atlantic coast of North Africa. Most of the population would become Muslims, and the city became a major centre of Islamic learning. For most of the ninth and tenth century, Samarkand was part of the Samanid Empire, a Muslim Iranian dynasty, before being ruled by a succession of different Turkic peoples.

In the early thirteenth century, a new force arrived at Samarkand: the Mongols. They were a nomadic people who came from the Eurasian Steppe, the belt of grassland that stretches 8,000 km (5,000 miles) from Eastern Europe to Manchuria.

CAFFA AND THE BLACK DEATH

The Silk Roads were the conduit for *Yersinia pestis*, the bacterium that caused the Black Death. The pandemic originated somewhere in Asia, and may have been introduced to Europe at Caffa (now Feodosia), a trading port in Crimea. A contemporary account suggests that the Mongols besieged it in 1346 and catapulted plague-infected corpses over the city walls, infecting the defenders. Some of those who escaped Caffa carried the plague into Italy, and from there it spread into North Africa and Europe. The outbreak lasted until 1351, killing over 100 million worldwide.

They were skilled riders and famed for their use of the composite bow, which they shot with deadly accuracy from horseback. For most of their history, the Mongols were not a united group but a collection of separate warring tribes. From 1190, Temujin (1162–1227), the son of a famed warrior, began to unify the tribes, using a mixture of force and diplomacy, which culminated in an assembly of chiefs hailing him as 'Genghis Khan' (universal leader) in 1206.

Although Genghis Khan and the Mongols were famed for their 'horde' of cavalry, they recruited military engineers, as well as spies to gather intelligence. This was because besieging cities for extended periods ran the risk of exhausting the local pasture, which would create supply problems. After raiding China and conquering neighbouring territories, in 1219 Genghis Khan set his sights on Muslim Central Asia. The following year, he arrived at Samarkand, slaughtering most of its garrison. The city surrendered, but it was still ransacked and pillaged. Such treatment was commonplace; the Mongols would treat cities that resisted them harshly to 'encourage' others to surrender peacefully.

After Genghis Khan died in 1227, he was succeeded by his son Ögedei (1186–1241), who extended the Mongol Empire into East Asia, making Korea a vassal state and attacking China, before turning west to campaign in Persia and the Caucasus. His rule meant that the Silk Road had a single ruler, and trade was eased. In 1236, the Mongols invaded Europe, advancing to Poland and Hungary before the death of Ögedei in 1241 halted their progress. It took seven years of civil war for a new, strong, khan, Möngke (1209–59), to emerge, but the unity of the Mongol Empire began to fragment. In the west it split off to form the Golden Horde, which established sovereignty over Russian principalities and forced them to pay tribute, dominating them until the Princes of Muscovy led a resistance that would throw off the 'Mongol Yoke' in the 1480s. In the Middle East, Mongols, having converted to Islam, founded a polity called the Ilkhanate, which disintegrated by the mid-fourteenth century. Finally, Genghis Khan's grandson Kublai Khan (1215–94) conquered much of China, and established himself as the first emperor of the Yuan dynasty, which lasted until 1368.

Samarkand became part of the fourth Mongol successor-state, the Chagatai Khanate. After the initial sack, the Mongols invested heavily in Samarkand to maximize its worth, encouraging skilled craftsmen to migrate there. In particular, they brought in workers to manage the neglected orchards and fields that surrounded the city. However, as Mongol authority collapsed in the fourteenth century, it left a power vacuum that was filled by other steppe peoples. One of the most fearsome was Timur, aka Tamerlane (1336–1405), a Muslim of Mongol and Turkic origin born in modern-day Uzbekistan. During the 1360s and 1370s, he conquered much of Central Asia and Persia. After he conquered Samarkand, he made it the capital of his Timurid Empire. He brought artisans and craftsmen from as far afield as Damascus to beautify his residences there. At his court were decorative golden trees as thick as a man's leg, with 'fruit' made of gems and pearls and 'leaves' made of gold. He also constructed a central high street lined with shops, and built numerous mosques. In 1398, Timur invaded India, destroying and looting Delhi, before turning west in 1400 to invade the Middle East and Anatolia. His next aim was to conquer China, but he died of fever before he could launch his plan. Samarkand remained part of the Timurid Empire, and was the site of a great observatory constructed in the 1420s (sadly, it was destroyed by religious fanatics in 1449). Ultimately, the Timurid Empire was a loosely organized polity based on extracting tribute, but was beset by a succession struggle and disappeared by the early sixteenth century. Samarkand then went into decline, and by the early eighteenth century had been mostly abandoned. However, by the mid-nineteenth century, it would be partially revived as a garrison town and administrative centre of the Russian Empire, which was expanding into Central Asia, and in 1888 it became a stop on the newly constructed Trans-Caspian Railway, making it an important trading hub once more. In 1924, Samarkand, and the rest of Uzbekistan, would formally become part of the Soviet Union before winning independence in 1991.

THE ITSUKUSHIMA SHRINE

The Itsukushima Shinto Shrine is one of the most treasured and revered sights in Japan. An enduring symbol of the artistry of the country's architecture, its vermillion buildings appear to float on water.

The Seto Inland Sea is a body of water that separates Honshū, Kyūshū and Shikoku, three of the five main islands of Japan. Off its northern shore, close to the city of Hiroshima, is a small island around 31 square km (12 square miles) in size. Named Itsukushima, it has become known as Miyajima, which means 'Shrine Island', because of the many temples located there.

Shinto, which means 'way of the gods', is Japan's main religion. Its most important feature is the worship of spirits (*kami*), which are present in nature, and also include venerated ancestors. They are acknowledged at large public shrines, which honour them and seek out their protection. The island of Itsukushima is dominated by Mount Misen. Covered partly by primeval forest, it is a sacred mountain famed for the miraculous events that are said to have taken place there. Given this, it was a natural choice for the site of a shrine, and one was built there in 593. It was rebuilt into its present form nearly six centuries later, under the patronage of the *daimyō* (feudal lord) Taira no Kiyomori (1118–81), who would rise to become de facto ruler of Japan, more powerful than even the emperor.

The Emperors of Japan had reigned since the seventh century BC, proclaiming themselves descendants of the most powerful *kami*; they were called *Tenno* ('heavenly sovereign'), signifying this. Despite this status, the emperors often found themselves reduced to figureheads. From the tenth century, noble families began to build up their strength by hiring paid warriors called samurai, and battling for dominance over the emperor, and control of the country. This led to a shift in power in Japan from the established nobility of the court in Kyoto (capital from 794 to 1869) to the provincial clans whose power was built on their manors and personal armies.

Kiyomori was a member of one of these clans, the Taira. Strong-willed and ruthless, he had risen to fame through defeating bandits and been given the governorship of Aki, a district that included Itsukushima. When he took up the post in 1146, a priest had appeared to him in a dream and told him to build a shrine on Itsukushima to ensure success and prosperity. It was conceived as a representation of paradise, and its elegant style mirrors that used in noble residences. The shrine's buildings are connected by 4-metre-wide (13 feet) walkways that extend to nearly 304 metre (1,000 feet) in length. Its most recognizable

feature is its *O-Torii* gate (the present one was built in 1875), which stands on stone slabs that make it appear to rise out of the water. The gate is situated on an axis that crosses through the purification room, a hall of worship, the offertory and the main sanctuary before continuing on to Mount Misen; when entering the shrine, it was customary to pass through the gate on a boat. Kiyomori was a great collector of religious art and sacred writings, and made many gifts to religious foundations. At Itsukushima he donated the *Heike nōkyō*, a collection of thirty-two scrolls on which he and other family members had copied out *sutras*. Each scroll was lavishly decorated with gold and richly illustrated. Kiyomori made numerous pilgrimages to Itsukushima to give thanks for his success. His visits had practical benefits, as they allowed him to survey his trading interests on the Inland Sea, and profit from the trade with China. To encourage commerce, he built new harbours and improved existing ones – greatly increasing maritime trade in western Japan.

The building of the Itsukushima Shrine coincided with Kiyomori's rise to power. In 1153, he became leader of the Taira clan, and in 1160 he defeated a rival family, the Minamoto. This established the Taira as the dominant force in Japan, and in 1167 Kiyomori was appointed chief minister, the highest office in the country. Symbolic of his clan's new status was the marriage of Kiyomuri's daughter to Emperor Takakura (1161–81) in 1171. Their son, Antoku, was born in 1178. Over the next two years, Kiyomori filled the imperial government with rivals and then imprisoned Takakura, forcing him to abdicate and pass the throne to Antoku (1178–85) in 1180. For many, this was unacceptable, and when Kiyomori died after a fever the following year, many rejoiced. By then the country was plunged into war between the Taira and Minamoto families. The Minamoto prevailed in 1185. When defeat became certain, Antoku's grandmother is said to have drowned the child emperor to prevent him falling into enemy hands. Another one of Takakura's sons became emperor but the Minamoto leader Yoritomo (1147–99) became the real ruler of Japan. In 1192, he was given the title of 'shogun', which was originally given to successful generals, but came to mean the person who ruled for the emperor. Shoguns remained in control of Japan until 1868, when the power of the emperor was restored.

URAGA HARBOUR

In 1543, Portuguese traders made contact with Japan, the first Europeans to do so. Westerners traded with Japan until the 1630s, when the shogunate enacted a policy, the Sakoku, which severely restricted foreign influence. This changed in 1853, when Commodore Matthew Perry (1794–1858) of the US Navy led a fleet of four steam-powered warships into Uraga harbour, at the entrance to Tokyo Bay. It was classic gunboat diplomacy; the Japanese government was forced to end the nation's isolation, and open up to the West.

Despite the fall from power of the Taira, Itsukushima remained important, with many nobles (as well as commoners, particularly fishermen, mariners and traders) worshipping there and patronizing it by donating treasures or funding buildings. The island itself came to be regarded as sacred, meaning no births and deaths were allowed there (expectant mothers were requested to travel to the mainland when the birth-date drew near). In 1571, the warlord Mōri Motonari (1497–1571) rebuilt the main shrine at Itsukushima, making it one of the largest in Japan. He did this as an act of penance – in 1555, when the country was beset by civil war, he had fought a battle on Itsukushima, defiling its sacred ground.

Japan began to modernize rapidly during the later nineteenth and early twentieth century, following its being forced to open up to the West in 1853. Japan became a colonial power, ruling an empire that included Korea, Taiwan and parts of Manchuria. Its territory continued to grow in the 1930s, and after Japan entered the Second World War on the Axis side in 1941, extending further into China, South-East Asia and the Pacific. Japan was finally defeated after the atomic bombings of Hiroshima and Nagasaki in August 1945. As part of its surrender, Emperor Hirohito (1901–89) renounced the imperial claim to divinity. Fortunately, Itsukushima survived the war intact and has been meticulously preserved. In 2004, the shrine was damaged by a typhoon, but since then it has been repaired and restored.

TENOCHTITLAN

During the fifteenth century, the Aztec Empire ruled much of Mexico from its capital city of Tenochtitlan. By 1521, both the empire, and Tenochtitlan itself, would face destruction following the arrival of a new power from Europe, Spain.

The Valley of Mexico is a large inland basin ringed by volcanic mountains; it had rich soil and salty lakes. A group called the Mexica migrated there from the north in around 1250, and initially settled in Chapultepec, a barren hill near a swamp. After quarrelling with a local king, they were forced to move again and wandered in search of a new home. According to legend, it was prophesied they would know they had reached the right location when they saw an eagle atop a cactus eating a snake. Around 1325, they saw the sign on an island in the middle of the swampy Lake Texcoco, leading them to found Tenochtitlan ('place of the cactus fruit') there.

The site was promising because the salty marshland provided wild plants and animals. It was ideal for a type of agriculture called *chinampa*; fields built on land reclaimed by plunging stakes into the lake bed and dumping soil on top. The population rapidly grew, and from 1367 they became a vassal of the Tepanecs, the dominant kingdom in the region at the time. In 1372, Tenochtitlan named its first king (*tlatoani*), a nobleman called Acamapichtli (d. 1391), who passed the throne on to his son Huitzilihuitl (d. 1415).

In around 1427, Huitzilihuitl's half-brother Itzcoatl (d. 1440) became king. The next year, he entered into a triple alliance with two other city-states, Texcoco and Tlacopan. Together they fought and defeated the Tepanecs, before conquering much of the Valley of Mexico and some adjacent areas. Tenochtitlan, and the Mexica, were the dominant force in the polity that became known as the Aztec Empire. The Mexica did not call themselves Aztecs, which means 'people from Aztlan' (the mythical place origin of them and many other groups in the region); but they have been commonly known by this appellation since the early nineteenth century.

With Tenochtitlan now an imperial capital, the city grew more grandiose, with the architectural transformation carrying on until the later fifteenth century. Following the model of

Teotihuacan (see opposite), its streets were laid out in a regular grid system, although with long canals intersecting the city. It was connected to the mainland by three chief causeways, broken at intervals to allow canoes to pass through them, and spanned by bridges that could be removed if the city came under attack. Across the western causeway was a masonry aqueduct that carried fresh spring water to the city, and a dyke was built to seal off Tenochtitlan from the saltier water in the east of the lake. In 1473, Tenochtitlan annexed the adjacent city of Tlatelolco (founded by another group of Mexica), which was on the same island just to the north. It was subsumed into Tenochtitlan, and was known for its marketplace, where up to 60,000 people were said to have gathered to buy and sell products including feathers, tobacco and slaves. Currencies used included cacao beans, cotton cloaks and gold-dust-filled quills; transactions and prices were overseen by inspectors, and thieves were punished by being beaten to death. At the centre of Tenochtitlan on an area of high ground was a sacred precinct enclosed by a structure called the 'Snake Wall'. It was the spiritual heart of the Aztec Empire, and from it the major avenues extended in the four cardinal directions. Inside it were at least seventy-eight buildings, the largest of which was the *Templo Mayor* (its Aztec name was *Huey Teocalli*, which means 'Great Temple'), a great pyramid jointly dedicated to Tlaloc, supreme deity of rain and farming, and Huitzilopochtli, god of war and patron of the city; its double stairs were stained red with the blood of human sacrifices. Below was a structure called the *tzompantli*, a skull rack that contained thousands of severed heads.

By the early sixteenth century, Tenochtitlan had a population of around 200,000, making it one of the largest cities in the world at the time. The power it represented was shattered at the hands of the Spanish conquistador Hernán Cortés (1485–1547). In 1518 the Governor of Cuba had given him permission to launch an expedition to Mexico. Cortés departed in February 1519, despite the governor rescinding his blessing for the mission at the final hour. Cortés had a force of about 500, but they were armed with gunpowder, weapons and had steel armour and cavalry – things unknown to the Aztecs.

TEOTHIHUACAN

Teothihuacan was located 48 km (30 miles) to the north-east of Tenochtitlan. It flourished between 100 BC and AD 600, reaching a population of over 100,000, and housed many impressive monuments. The exact identity of its builders is unclear, and it is uncertain why it was abandoned and fell into ruin from the seventh century BC. Indeed, its original name is also unknown: Teothihuacan (which means 'birthplace of the gods') was the name given to it by the Aztecs, for whom it was an important pilgrimage site.

After landing in Mexico, Cortés marched on Tenochtitlan, winning several victories en route, and entered the city on 8 November. The reigning king, Moctezuma II (*c.* 1466–1520), initially welcomed the Spanish and showered them with gifts, hoping to defeat them later, but soon found himself held hostage by Cortés, who sought to make him a puppet ruler. The following April, Cortés left Tenochtitlan to meet an expedition sent from Cuba to bring him to heel, leaving a lieutenant and a force of eighty in the city. On 22 May, the Spanish massacred hundreds of Aztec nobles as they were celebrating a religious festival, leading to a local revolt. The Spanish found themselves besieged for nearly a month, escaping under cover of a midnight rainstorm on 30 June (around this time Moctezuma II was killed, possibly at the hands of his own subjects). However, they had left behind smallpox, a disease the population had no natural resistance to, and an epidemic swept the city, killing the new king Cuitláhuac (*c.* 1476–1520), who reigned for only eighty days. In May 1521, Cortés returned to Tenochtitlan with Spanish reinforcements and a coalition of local allies eager to defeat the Aztecs. He laid siege to the city, cutting off its water and food supply, and gradually advanced. The final assault took place on 13 August; King Cuauhtémoc (*c.* 1495 – *c.* 1525) was taken captive, and the victorious forces spent four days sacking the city and massacring its people. The Aztec Empire was gone; Tenochtitlan lay in waste. Cortés became the first viceroy of New Spain, the colonial territory that would rule modern-day Mexico (as well as territories to the north and south) until 1821. Although it lay in ruins, Tenochtitlan was chosen as the site of its capital, which developed into Mexico City.

HUIS TER BEURSE

. . . .

Some of the earliest roots of Western capitalism can be traced back to the medieval era; one of the greatest centres of commerce at the time was Bruges (or Brugge), which welcomed merchants from across Europe. Many gathered at the Huis ter Beurse, an inn where they met and conducted business.

The Flemish city of Bruges, which received its charter in 1128, stood at the crossroads of the medieval economy, with trade links to the Baltic, Mediterranean and North Sea. The mainstay of the region's economy was cloth manufacture: Bruges sold the textiles that were produced in towns like Ypres, Ghent and Douai. Bruges could act as a commercial hub because it had a tidal outlet that gave it direct access to the North Sea, meaning it could bring in shipments of wool from England.

Numerous inns opened to cater to the merchants who came to Bruges. They offered food, drink and lodging but were also forums for swapping news about prices, rates of exchange and the latest political developments. They also had links with money changers, and began to take deposits from their guests, as well as extend credit to them, As such, these inns in Bruges became crucial facilitators of trade at a time when there were no formal banking mechanisms. These inns would replace the temporary trading fairs that had previously been the main forums for merchants to gather.

The Hanseatic League was also drawn to Bruges, which became the main terminus of its east–west trading route that stretched all the way to Novgorod in north-western Russia. It established a *kontor* (trading post) there and made it the staple market for the sale of its goods in the Low Countries. From the later thirteenth century, Italian merchants, starting with the Genoese, began to arrive in Bruges. They largely established themselves at the Beursplein, a square at the end of the Vlamingstraat, in the heart of the city. It was named after the van der Beurse (literally, 'of the purse') family. They were brokers and innkeepers who had risen to prominence from the mid-thirteenth century, establishing a complex of houses on the square that bore their name. Their inn, known as the Huis ter Beurse, bore their symbol of three purses carved into stone; and it became an important meeting place for Italian merchants.

HANSEATIC LEAGUE

From the mid-thirteenth century, over 200 northern German towns and cities would come together to control and regulate commerce along the Baltic Sea. They formed an alliance called the Hanseatic League (from Hanse, the German for 'association') that came to monopolize the Baltic trade. The central hub was Lübeck, where the code that governed the League was formulated. Facing competition from the likes of Poland, Russia and Sweden, the League declined from the later fifteenth century and held its final meeting in 1669.

The van der Beurse family left Bruges at the end of the fourteenth century, migrating to Antwerp, which was far better positioned to trade with Germany and could still access the North Sea via the River Scheldt. Their house was sold to the Venetians, who used it as the headquarters of their trading colony in Bruges until 1505, when it became an inn once more. The flight of the van der Beurses from Bruges was symptomatic of the city's decline over the fifteenth century, as many merchants left the city. It was no longer an attractive location because its inlet to the North Sea silted up, robbing it of direct access to the coast. Even the Hanseatic League, which had been such a supporter of Bruges in its heyday, effectively abandoned the city by removing its status as their main market in north-western Europe in 1477.

With Bruges in decline, Antwerp succeeded it to became the most important economic centre in north-western Europe. The mercantile legacy of Bruges would live on there. In 1531, when galleries were built in Antwerp's open squares to provide shelter for merchants, they became known as the 'bourse' after the inn in Bruges. Bills of exchange, as well as commodities, were bought and sold there. Later on, organized trading venues or markets across Europe would often become known as a 'bourse'. Like Bruges, Antwerp would also lose its status, although for a different reason. By the mid-sixteenth century, most of the Low Countries were under the control of the Spanish Habsburgs, who clashed with the local population over their attempts to impose centralized authority on the region. In addition, Protestantism had won many adherents in the Low Countries, further straining relations with the staunchly Catholic Habsburgs. In 1568, a rebellion broke out against them. Antwerp, which largely supported the revolt, was caught up in the fighting; it was sacked by the Spanish in 1576 and permanently captured by them in 1585. Thousands of Protestants fled, and the Dutch rebels blocked the Scheldt, cutting off its access to the North Sea. In spite of this, Antwerp did retain a measure of economic importance, but it was soon eclipsed by Amsterdam. The Dutch city welcomed many of the citizens who had fled Antwerp, as well as Jews who had been expelled from Portugal. It became the centre of the maritime empire established by the Dutch Republic, and one of the most dynamic trade entrepôts in the world.

Following its medieval 'golden age', Bruges declined in economic importance. It retained its medieval old town, which stood as a monument to its former glory. In 1907, the port of Zeebrugge, which was connected to Bruges by a canal, was opened. This helped revive Bruges's fortunes somewhat, as well as encouraging tourism. The city was occupied by German forces in both world wars, but was fortunately spared destruction, and its historic centre, including the Huis ter Beurse, was made a UNESCO World Heritage Site in 2000.

VENICE

In the medieval Mediterranean, the greatest trading power was the Republic of Venice. It established trading routes that extended all the way to India and China, tapping into the Silk Road. The Venetians also won possessions elsewhere in Italy and on the eastern Adriatic coast, as well as ruling some Greek islands and Cyprus. They lost most of their overseas possessions in the sixteenth century, and in 1797 the republic was disbanded and partitioned between France and Austria.

GYEONGBOKGUNG

· ·

The Yi dynasty ruled Korea for over five centuries, establishing a sophisticated administrative structure while encouraging learning and trade; they also founded a new capital in Seoul, the location of their main royal palace, Gyeongbokgung.

The Goryeo kingdom had dominated the Korean Peninsula since its foundation in 918, but by the later fourteenth century its position had been undermined by warfare and Mongol incursions. With the country in chaos, in 1392, General Yi Seong-gye (1335–1408) seized power. Taking the regnal name Taejo, he established a new dynasty and renamed the kingdom Joseon. He justified his actions by claiming that the previous dynasty had been immoral, meaning they had lost the mandate of heaven, which he now claimed.

Taejo and his sons enacted reforms that would have a long-term impact on Korean culture and society. They were proponents of neo-Confucianism, a school of thought that was built on the ethics of social harmony and order that Confucius had encouraged, but with a greater focus on rationalism and secularism. Taejo therefore confiscated the landholdings of Buddhist temples and redistributed them to his supporters.

In 1394, Taejo moved his capital to Hanyang. It also became known as Seoul, which originates from the Korean for 'capital city' (the name was not officially changed until 1948). In 1395, Taejo began construction of a palace there: Gyeongbokgung

('Palace Greatly Blessed by Heaven'), which would become the foremost residence of his dynasty. It was an extensive complex with over 400 buildings, the largest of the five palaces the Yi built in their capital. It was built in a north–south configuration, surrounded by a stone wall with gates at the four cardinal points. The main entry was in the south, and known as the 'triple rainbow gate' for the three arched portals built into its granite base. Hanyang was built into a grand capital. Over 100,000 forced labourers were drafted in to build the city on a grid (modelled on Chinese imperial capitals), and construct palaces, buildings, walls and gates.

The greatest of the Joseon kings was Taejo's grandson Sejong (1397–1450), who came to the throne in 1418. He was supported by a sophisticated bureaucracy. Administrative officials were graded into nine ranks, subdivided into junior and senior levels, with laws governing their behaviour and status. A department called the Censorate guided the moral conduct of the nation, and closely monitored the public and private lives of officials. Government jobs were decided by public examination, where prospective recruits were tested on their knowledge of Classical Chinese and Confucian texts. Symbolic of the order the Yi wished to created were the *hopae* – identification tags, stamped with the seal of a government official, that all men over fifteen had to make and carry. In practice, this ambitious scheme, which was instituted in 1413, was not always enforced.

Although an absolute monarch, Sejong often consulted with his subjects so they could bring their problems to him. One of his main aims was to improve agriculture; he gathered

HANGUL

As part of his efforts to strengthen the nation, Sejong established a body of scholars and researchers called the Hall of Worthies. Its greatest achievement was a new alphabet. Before Sejong, Koreans had used Chinese characters to write, which were not well suited to their language. Sejong oversaw the creation of a new, simpler, alphabet called Hangul (meaning 'great script' or 'Korean script'). Promulgated in 1446, it has only twenty-four letters, which made it easier to learn and use.

together learned men to write a handbook containing information for farmers so they could be more productive. It was distributed to regional officials in 1429; partly as a result, more land was brought under cultivation, with the amount farmed doubling from 1400 to 1550. Sejong unified his realms by installing a water clock and standardized measuring devices at Gyeongbokgung (which he continued to expand) that acted as a national model. He left behind eighteen sons, contributing to a great succession struggle after his death in 1450, which weakened the kingdom.

Gyeongbokgung underwent severe tribulations during the later sixteenth century. In 1553, it was devastated by a fire and required extensive rebuilding. Worse was to follow in 1592 when Japanese forces, armed with Western firearms, invaded the Korean Peninsula. With their forces overwhelmed, the Joseon kings abandoned Hanyang. Left alone in the capital, slaves rebelled, burning government buildings as part of an attempt to destroy the registers that recorded their unfree status. A combination of this arson and damage done by the invaders meant that Gyeongbokgung was destroyed. The war continued until 1598, when the Joseon, with the support of China, forced the Japanese to withdraw. The royal family chose another palace in Hanyang, Changdeokgung, as their residence, and Gyeongbokgung was abandoned.

Gyeongbokgung was reconstructed from 1865 to 1869; during the reign of Gojong (1851–1919). The rebuilt palace had over 300 buildings and 7,225 rooms, and once again became the seat of power for the Joseon kings. However, Gyeongbokgung would be caught up in Japanese plans to extend their power over the Korean Peninsula. In 1895, one of Gojong's wives, Myeongseong (1851–95), who had been an outspoken opponent of Japanese influence, was assassinated in Gyeongbokgung. The crime had been carried out by Japanese agents who had infiltrated the palace. Gojong and his heir abandoned Gyeongbokgung and relocated their court to another palace, Deoksugung. There, to display the country's independence and protect its sovereignty from Japan, Gojong proclaimed the Korean Empire and adopted an imperial title in 1897. The move did little to stem Japanese encroachment, and in 1905 they established a protectorate over Korea before annexing it five years later, formally ending the rule of the Yi.

Gyeongbokgung faced severe depredations. In 1915, many of the halls there were torn down and replaced with temporary structures for an industrial exhibition. To symbolize their power, the Japanese colonial authorities built their central administrative building near the main gate of the palace (it was not demolished until 1995). By the time Japanese rule ended in 1945, only a handful of the buildings in Gyeongbokgung remained wholly intact.

Today Gyeongbokgung is the location of the National Palace Museum of Korea, which was established in 1908 and houses artefacts and treasures from the country's royal past. Also within the grounds are the National Folk Museum of Korea and replicas of Buddhist temples from across the country (this is somewhat controversial given the Yi dynasty's favouring of neo-Confucianism). The South Korean government has invested heavily in rebuilding Gyeongbokgung; the ongoing restoration is an important symbol of national pride in their history.

CUSCO

· · · · · · · · · · · ·

The Inca Empire was the culmination of three millennia of complex civilizations that emerged in the Andes. Locally known as *Tawantinsuyu* ('The Four Parts Together'), it covered 4,000 km (2,500 miles) of western South America and had a peak population of over 10 million, ruled from its capital, Cusco.

The Inca Empire, early sixteenth century AD

According to legend, the Inca people originated from the village of Paqari-tampu 24 km (15 miles) south of Cusco, where there were three caves. From the middle one emerged the mythical founder of the Inca dynasty, Manco Cápac, along with his three brothers and four sisters, while their people came from the caves on either side. Manco Cápac established dominance over his brothers and led the people across the Andes in search of a home. He was known as the *Sapa Inca* ('The Only Inca'), and all subsequent leaders traced descent from him. Eventually, the Inca settled in Cusco, where they dislodged the local inhabitants. Regardless of the veracity of their creation myth, the Inca settled Cusco by the twelfth century. It was situated at the upper end of a verdant mountain valley at an elevation of over 3,353 m (11,000 feet), and watered by mountain springs. Its name has been interpreted in numerous ways, including meaning 'rocky outcrop', 'dried-up lake bed' or 'centre', or being a reference to a stone territorial marker called a *cozco*.

After founding Cusco, the Inca established dominance over the valley, defeating neighbouring villages and compelling them to pay tribute. In the early to mid-fourteenth century, the Inca ventured out of the Cusco valley, defeating several tribes. They became an imperial power under Sapa Inca Pachakuti (1418–71/2), and expanded south towards Lake Titicaca and north to modern-day Ecuador. During his reign, Cusco reached its final form, sprawling across surrounding settlements and reaching a population of around 150,000. The city's core was forty hectares in size, and was probably laid out by Pachakuti himself, allegedly in the shape of a puma. Its inhabitants were supplied with water by stone-lined channels running along its paved streets, and its storehouses were refilled every four days.

At the centre of Cusco was a great plaza, which the Huatanay river bisected into two sectors: the *Awkaypata* ('place of crying') and *Kusipata* ('place of rejoicing'). The area was used for ceremonial events such as investing new rulers. The

Awkaypata was covered in sand from the Pacific coast in which gold and silver figurines were buried, and frequently hosted the mummified remains of dead rulers (or their icons), which were seated according to rank. On the northern outskirts of Cusco was the Saqsawaman, which overlooked the city and had massive terrace walls. It was a combination of citadel, shrine and ceremonial centre. As imperial capital, Cusco was the residence of the Sapa Inca and his family. Each ruler built himself a new palace that was maintained as his eternal resting place after death; his furnishings remained in place and his mummy or effigy was tended to by servants. In an attempt to tie together the realm, the chiefs of conquered tribes were supposed to keep houses in Cusco and spend four months a year there, with one son maintaining continuous residence.

Cusco played a crucial role in the Inca religion. Coricancha, the city's largest religious building, was dedicated to their patron deity, the sun god Inti. Under Pachakuti's patronage it was extensively rebuilt and decorated with gold plate. The Inca Empire would reach its greatest size (over 1.8 million square km or over 700,000 square miles) in the early sixteenth century during the reign of Pachakuti's grandson Huayna Capac (1464/8–1524), who oversaw a centralized government and had a well-trained standing army of around 200,000. The arrival of Europeans would dangerously destabilize the Inca Empire, leading to its eventual destruction.

Francisco Pizarro (*c.* 1475–1541) was the illegitimate son of a soldier, and had left Spain in 1509 and settled in Panama. He had led expeditions to Inca territory in 1526 and 1529 and saw their huge wealth, leading him to launch a full-scale invasion (albeit with just 168 men) in 1532. Despite the small size of his force, Pizarro had the advantage of steel and iron weapons and armour, gunpowder and horses. Furthermore, the Sapa Inca Atahualpa (c. 1502–33) had only recently established himself as ruler after defeating his brother in a costly civil war. Pizarro met Atahualpa at Cajamarca on 16 November. He ambushed the Inca forces, killing over 7,000 and capturing Atahualpa, demanding a ransom for him. Although it was paid, Pizarro considered that keeping Atahualpa alive was risky, and executed him on 26 July 1533. This effectively marked the end of the Inca Empire.

Pizarro then led his men on Cusco, occupying it on 15 November. Coricancha was stripped of valuables and given to the Dominican Order, who built a monastery around it. Cusco was officially refounded as a Spanish city, although Pizarro decided to establish his capital on the coast, founding the city of Lima. Pizarro installed Manco Inca (c. 1533 – c. 1544), one of Atahualpa's cousins, as a puppet royal who was detained in Cusco. He tried to flee for the first time in November 1535, but was recaptured and detained, and allegedly urinated on and had his eyelashes burned. He escaped the following April, after telling his captors he was going into the countryside to perform ceremonies, and that he would return with a life-sized golden statue of his father. Manco Inca would lead an uprising against Spanish rule, arriving in Cusco in May 1536 with over 200,000 soldiers. The Spanish survived the ten-month siege, despite having only a few hundred troops and around 1,000 local allies. Manco Inca retreated to the jungles of the interior, where he founded a state that survived until 1572.

No longer the capital, Cusco went into decline. Parts of the city had been burned during the siege, and the Spanish dismantled much of its architecture – for example, demolishing most of the Saqsawaman (although many of the stones in its walls were too large to move and remain in place to this day). To de-sanctify the *Awkaypata*, they removed the sand that covered it and used it in construction. The space became the Plaza de Armas and was fronted by two cathedrals. After Cusco was severely damaged by an earthquake in 1650, much of the city was rebuilt in the Baroque style, meaning that today there are only a few remnants of its past as the capital of a great empire.

KOSOVO POLJE

. . . .

The Battle of Kosovo (1389) marked the beginning of Ottoman domination of the Balkans, and would retain an important significance in the region for centuries afterwards.

The nascent Ottoman Empire won its first territory in Europe when its forces occupied a fortress on the Gallipoli Peninsula in 1352. With the Byzantine Empire in steep decline, the Ottomans had conquered the city of Adrianople (now Edirne) by 1369, opening the way for further expansion into the Balkans. By this time, the Balkans were populated by the Slavs, an Indo-European people who had settled the region over the sixth and seventh century. They had established several

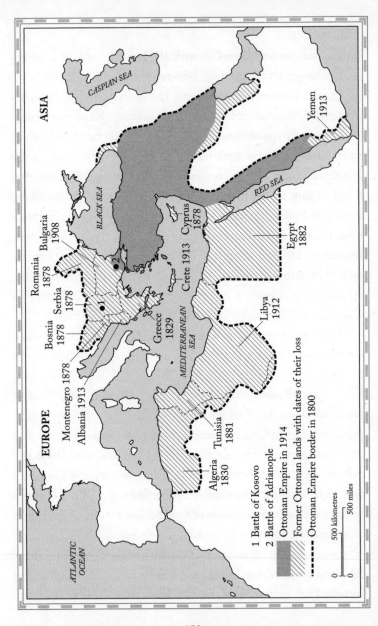

EUROPE

ASIA

CASPIAN SEA

BLACK SEA

RED SEA

MEDITERRANEAN SEA

ATLANTIC OCEAN

Yemen 1913

Egypt 1882

Cyprus 1878

Crete 1913

Libya 1912

Greece 1829

Tunisia 1881

Algeria 1830

Bulgaria 1908

Romania 1878

Serbia 1878

Bosnia 1878

Montenegro 1878

Albania 1913

1 Battle of Kosovo
2 Battle of Adrianople

Ottoman Empire in 1914

Former Ottoman lands with dates of their loss

Ottoman Empire border in 1800

0   500 kilometres
0   500 miles

· 150 ·

states, and converted to Christianity, but the lack of a strong central power left them vulnerable to the Ottomans.

From 1385 to 1387, Sultan Murad I (1326–89) won a series of victories that saw the Ottomans push into northern Greece and southern Macedonia. However, in 1388 their attempt to conquer Bosnia was thwarted when they were defeated at the Battle of Bileća. Murad I responded to the setback by gathering a large army, which included some allied Slavs, and marching west the following year. The most powerful Slav leader was Prince Lazar Hrebeljanović (1329–89), who ruled a large state in Serbia. He organized a coalition to defeat the Ottomans, which included Serbians, Bosnians, Bulgarians, Wallachians, Albanians and even a contingent of Knights Hospitaller (a Catholic military order founded during the Crusades).

The two armies met at Kosovo Polje (the Field of Blackbirds), north-west of the city of Pristina, on 15 June. Accounts of the battle vary widely, but it was probably a stalemate in which both sides suffered huge losses. They included both leaders: Murad I was killed by a Serbian who had tricked his way into his presence, while Lazar was captured and executed (possibly after being betrayed by an ally). The Ottomans, who could still call on significant reinforcements from Anatolia, were better able to weather the losses suffered. The Serbians did not have the same manpower, and the loss of Lazar robbed them of their most charismatic leader.

Even though Kosovo had been inconclusive, for many Serbians it went down in national memory as a major defeat that signalled the beginning of the Ottoman yoke. In later centuries,

Kosovo became a rallying cry for the Serbians who wished to forge their own national independence. The site of the battlefield became known as Gazimestan (derived from the Arabic *ghazi*, which means 'hero', and the Serbian *mesto*, which means 'place').

Murad I's son Bayezid I (1360–1403) succeeded his father, and made Serbia an Ottoman vassal, marrying Lazar's daughter to seal the agreement. By the end of the fourteenth century, the Ottomans controlled most of the southern Balkans. As long as territories paid taxation and were loyal, they were permitted a fairly high degree of autonomy. Christianity remained the majority religion in most areas, although many converted to Islam, particularly in Albania and Bosnia. The region of Kosovo became an Ottoman vilayet (province) – among its population the largest group were Albanian Muslims. During the fifteenth and sixteenth century, the Ottoman Empire went from strength to strength. In 1444, it defeated an allied Polish–Hungarian army, paving the way for expansion into Bosnia and Herzegovina. Belgrade was captured in 1521, and in 1526 the Hungarians were destroyed at the Battle of Mohács, The Ottoman drive westward was halted in 1529, when they were turned back after failing to capture Vienna.

The Ottomans faced periodic revolts and rising nationalist sentiment in the Balkans, and by the end of the nineteenth century Greece, Montenegro, Romania and Serbia had all become independent, while Bulgaria was autonomous (and declared formal independence in 1908). The Battle of Kosovo retained an enormous significance to the pan-Slavists, people who believed that all of the Balkans should be unified into a single state, free of any external influence. The subject of their ire was the Austro-Hungarian Empire, which ruled Croatia and Bosnia–Herzegovina. So, when Archduke Franz Ferdinand (1863–1914), heir to the Austro-Hungarian throne, visited Sarajevo in 1914 on the anniversary of the Battle of Kosovo, it was highly controversial. A member of Young Bosnia, a pan-Slav group supported by Serbia, assassinated Franz Ferdinand and his wife, unleashing a chain of events that culminated in the outbreak of the First World War.

After that war, the Kingdom of Serbs, Croats and Slovenes (later renamed Yugoslavia) was founded in the Balkans, fulfilling the ambitions of pan-Slavists. It included Kosovo, and in 1924 a monument was built at Gazimestan, and was the site of annual commemorations. The Kingdom of Yugoslavia lasted until 1941, when the Axis powers invaded, occupied and partitioned it. After the Second World War, it became a federalized socialist state led by Josip Broz Tito (1892–1980), who ruled until his death in 1980.

The loss of Tito, and economic decline in the 1980s, placed the federation under strain. In 1989, Slobodan Milošević (1941–2006), leader of the Republic of Serbia, addressed a large crowd at Gazimestan (where a new monument had been built in 1953). He stated that six centuries before, Serbia had fought there to save the rest of Europe from Ottoman domination, and that therefore it should always retain control of Kosovo, even though many of its inhabitants wanted independence. His speech also hinted at the possibility of war to defend his ambitions for Serbia; such rhetoric was symptomatic of the rising nationalism that helped bring about the collapse of Yugoslavia in 1991. Over the next four years, the Balkans collapsed into warfare, which was accompanied by numerous massacres and ethnic cleansing.

TITO'S CAVE

During the Second World War, the Axis conquered Yugoslavia in 1941, but there was widespread domestic resistance. One of the main groups was the communist Partisans, who were led by Tito. On 25 May 1944, Axis forces assaulted Tito's headquarters, a cave in the hills outside the Bosnian town of Drvar. Tito escaped, and the next year became leader of the newly established Socialist Federal Republic of Yugoslavia.

After the war, Milošević became president of the Republic of Serbia and Montenegro, which included Kosovo. In 1998, he attacked the pro-independence rebels in Kosovo, leading to bloodshed and population displacement. To prevent a humanitarian crisis, in 1999, NATO intervened and forced Milošević to withdraw. He was later voted out of office and extradited to The Hague to stand trial for war crimes, but died in 2006 before a verdict was delivered. Meanwhile, Kosovo was placed under a UN administration that ended with it declaring independence in 2008.

6

The Early Modern Era

THE ALHAMBRA

From the eighth to the fifteenth century, Muslim rulers reigned over parts of Iberia, sometimes controlling almost all of the peninsula. Their most long-standing presence was in Granada, where the ruling emirs built the Alhambra, a palace that represented the aesthetic delight of Islamic architecture.

In 711, the Umayyad Caliphate invaded Iberia, establishing a territory they called al-Andalus. Following a civil war, the Umayyads were overthrown by the Abbasids. Muslim rule in Iberia continued under an Umayyad prince who established the independent Emirate of Córdoba in 756. It would collapse into civil war during the early eleventh century, splitting up into small states called *taifa*s. This created a power vacuum filled by Moroccan Berber dynasties (first the Almoravids, then the

Almohads), who enjoyed overlordship in Islamic Iberia from 1090 to 1212.

Christian powers had survived in the north of Iberia, and fought a series of wars called the Reconquista to push back the Islamic rulers. In doing so, they established several independent kingdoms, which used their military power to force the *taifa* kings to pay them tribute. In 1212, the allied Christian armies won a great victory at Las Navas de Tolosa over the Almohads, laying the foundation for the removal of Muslim rule from southern Spain. The most powerful Christian Spanish kingdom was Castile, which from 1217 to 1252 was ruled by Ferdinand III (*c.* 1199–1252), who oversaw the capture of Seville and Córdoba. He allowed one remnant of al-Andalus to remain: the Emirate of Grenada. It was founded by Abu Abdullah Muhammad ibn Yusuf ibn Nasr (1195–1273), a *taifa* king who had supported Ferdinand III. The Nasrid dynasty that he established ruled Granada until 1492.

The Emirate of Granada covered a coastal fringe as well as some mountainous territory inland. The emirate's poor land meant it had to import grain from North Africa, although it profited from exporting luxury goods such as silk, sugar and dried fruit. Castile, to the north, forced Granada to pay an annual tribute of gold. If it was late, they carried out punitive border raids, destroying farms and settlements. To establish himself in Granada, Muhammad I decided to build himself a palace, the *Qal'at al-Hamra*, which means the red fort (after the colour of the walls made from the clay soil of the surrounding area), and was contracted to 'Alhambra'. He chose a plateau overlooking the city that had been the site of a small fortress (as well as built on by the Romans). The building work would take centuries, and his successors continuously added to and renovated the complex.

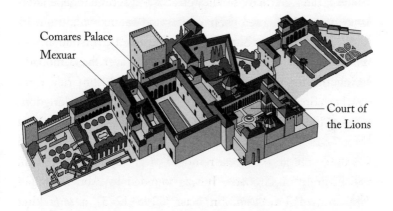

Comares Palace
Mexuar
Court of the Lions

The Alhambra's outer enclosure was completed by the end of the thirteenth century; its thick walls had a perimeter of around 2.25 km (1.4 miles), with twenty-two towers. Also added by this time was the aqueduct – the supply of running water was crucial for the Alhambra's many fountains and bathhouse. There are three main sections of the Alhambra: the Mexuar, the Comares Palace and the Court of the Lions. The Mexuar was built during the 1320s, and was used by the Nasrids for public business. The Comares Palace was built during the mid-fourteenth century and was used for more private audiences as well as the reception of ambassadors. Finally, the Court of the Lions was added during the later fourteenth century and acted as the private apartments of the Nasrid dynasty. All of these buildings were richly decorated throughout, with the complex geometric patterns distinctive to Islamic art. To the east of the Alhambra was the Generalife (a corruption of *Jinnah al-'Arif*, which means 'Garden of the Architect'), a summer palace sited amid ornamental gardens, pavilions and fountains laid out in the 1310s and 1320s. The westernmost part of the complex was the Alcazaba, a citadel which was variously a barracks, military storehouse and prison.

PALOS DE LA FRONTERA

On 3 August 1492, three ships, the *Pinta*, *Niña* and *Santa María*, left the Andalusian port of Palos de la Frontera. The expedition, led by Columbus, sought a new sea route to Asia. After crossing the Atlantic, the ships arrived in the Caribbean on 12 October (Columbus still believed they had reached Asia). They returned to Palos de la Frontera on 15 March 1493; their voyage would lay the foundations of Spain's global empire and the European colonization of the Americas.

The Nasrid dynasty, which had been mired in civil war and fighting incursions from the north for a decade, came to an end on 2 January 1492, when Muhammad XII (*c.* 1460–

1533) surrendered to Isabella I of Castile (1451–1504) and her husband Ferdinand II of Aragon (1452–1516), whose marriage had laid the foundation of the unification of Spain. The Alhambra was designated a royal palace by Ferdinand and Isabella. They found it was fairly dilapidated and hired Muslim craftsmen to restore it, as well as ordering a Christian chapel be built there. There they would receive Christopher Columbus (1451–1506) and endorse and finance his voyage across the Atlantic. This led to the foundation of the worldwide empire their grandson Emperor Charles V (1500–58) inherited in 1516. Charles first visited the Alhambra in 1526. Although he admired its artistry, it was not convenient to use as a royal palace, so he commissioned a new residence to be built for him in its grounds (destroying parts of the original Alhambra in the process). It was never fully completed and the work was abandoned after a century.

By the mid-seventeenth century, the Alhambra was in a sorry state, and its palaces were being used to hold prisoners and invalid soldiers. During the Napoleonic era, it suffered further depredations as French soldiers stripped the unfinished palace of Charles V of its timber to use as kindling and blew up eight of the perimeter towers. When the Duke of Wellington (1769–1852) arrived in Granada during the Peninsular War, he added his own touch by planting English elm trees in the park surrounding the Alhambra. For much of the nineteenth century, the Alhambra was used to keep animals. Weeds grew among its buildings, and earthquakes and fires did further damage. Since the mid-nineteenth century, the Alhambra has been the subject of near-continuous renovation and conservation work, which has helped to bring its glory to life once more.

BELÉM PARISH

· ·

On the western edge of Lisbon, at the entrance to its port, is the parish of Santa Maria de Belém. It became inextricably linked with Portugal's rise as a colonial and trading power during the fifteenth and sixteenth century.

In 1147, Afonso I (*c.* 1109–85), the first King of Portugal, captured Lisbon from its Muslim rulers after a four-month siege. He was assisted by a contingent of crusaders from north-western Europe who had landed in Portugal after bad weather prevented them from sailing directly to the Holy Land. The city would go on to become the capital of Portugal and play a pivotal role in its history as an administrative centre and trading hub. Lisbon was built on the slopes of two hills overlooking both the River Tagus and the Atlantic Ocean, and had the best natural deepwater harbour and protected anchorage on Europe's Atlantic coast.

The Portuguese kings, aware that their native territory was thinly populated and lacking in natural resources or good farming land, were keen to promote maritime trade and exploration. During the early fifteenth century, they began to look beyond Europe for wealth and glory. In 1415, Portugal

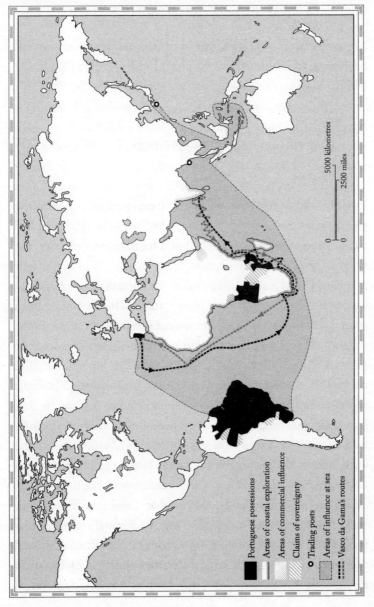

The Portuguese overseas empire, sixteenth to nineteenth century

Portuguese possessions	
Areas of coastal exploration	
Areas of commercial influence	
Claims of sovereignty	
Trading posts	
Areas of influence at sea	
Vasco da Gama's routes	

5000 kilometres
2500 miles

captured the North African city of Ceuta. This was just the beginning of Portugal's overseas expansion. The settlement of Madeira began from 1420, and was followed by the discovery of the Azores in 1427. Due to their subtropical climate, both became the location of plantations, most importantly of sugar. From the mid-fifteenth century, Portuguese merchants and explorers became active in West Africa, establishing trading posts and mapping the coastline as far as the Cape of Good Hope. During this time, they also discovered the Cape Verde archipelago, and settled the islands in 1462. For Portugal, this exploration went hand-in-hand with profit. They were the first Europeans to enslave Africans, transporting them from their homelands and forcing them to labour on their plantations.

There was a still greater prize that Portugal sought: a sea route around Africa, so they could trade directly with India. This would give them access to the lucrative goods, particularly spices, of Asia, thus bypassing the Muslim merchants who controlled the overland routes to the region. From 1487 to 1488, Bartolomeu Dias (1450–1500) led an expedition that sailed around the Cape of Good Hope, the southernmost tip of Africa. In 1497, Vasco da Gama (c. 1460–1524), a minor noble with little seafaring experience, was selected by King Manuel I (1469–1521) to lead an expedition that would build on Dias's. Da Gama and his men spent their last night in Portugal in Belém, praying in a hermitage that was especially favoured by seafarers. Fortune smiled on their voyage – da Gama sighted the Indian coast on 18 May 1498, and the first of his ships returned home in July 1499. The Portuguese would go on to establish several trading posts in India, as well as in East Africa. Meanwhile, they also established themselves as a colonial power in South America, after the explorer Pedro Álvares Cabral (1467/8–1520) made landfall in Brazil and claimed it for the Portuguese Crown.

DIU

By 1509, Portugal was facing opposition as it sought to establish itself in India. The Sultan of Gujarat and the King of Calicut, joined by the Mamluk Sultanate of Egypt, amassed a fleet to dislodge the Portuguese once and for all. The decisive battle took place off Diu, a port in western India. Although outnumbered, the larger and more powerful Portuguese ships devastated their enemies, winning a major victory that assured their control of trade routes across the Indian Ocean for a century.

In 1502, Manuel began construction of a monastery in Belém, built around the site where da Gama and his men had prayed before leaving. Financed partly by a tax on spices from Asia, the Monastery of Jerónimos was given to the Order of Hieronymites. Manuel hoped its monks would pray for his soul, as well as the success of the mariners who left Portugal.

Taking a century to complete, it was built in the 'Manueline' style, which is distinguished by its use of exuberant use of maritime and exotic themes in its rich decorations. Da Gama, who had died in India in 1524 serving as the Portuguese viceroy, was entombed there. Close to the monastery is the Tower of Belém, which was built to guard the approaches to the Tagus River estuary. Work on the tower, which was located on a rocky outcrop close to the riverbank, began in 1515 on the orders of Manuel I, and was completed in 1521. Dedicated to St Vincent, the patron of Lisbon, the limestone tower served as a garrison, prison, watchtowers and surrounding bulwark. It is an example of the Manueline style, as well as having Roman, Venetian and Moroccan influences.

During the sixteenth century, Portugal was dislodged as the dominant colonial power in the Indian Ocean by the English and Dutch, and it also faced competition in West Africa. In 1580, a succession crisis led to the Portuguese crown being claimed by the King of Spain. It was not until 1640 that Portugal and its empire were once more ruled by its own royal dynasty. Bélem continued to play an important role. In 1726, King John V (1689–1750) began construction of a palace with a distinctive pink exterior in Belém. It was renovated and extended in the nineteenth century, with intricate interiors and gardens added, and has been the official residence of the President of Portugal since 1911.

Disaster struck Lisbon in 1755, when a major earthquake and an accompanying tsunami devastated the city. Over 50,000 people died and only swift action from the government prevented a major outbreak of disorder and disease. Belém was spared most of the destruction, and it mostly survived intact. Many resettled in tents and temporary structures in the parish and surrounding areas, including the royal family, which following the earthquake moved the court to Ajuda, Belém's neighbouring parish, in a complex that included a large tent and wooden buildings. Much of the structure at Ajuda was destroyed by fire in 1794, and a new stone palace was begun the following year. In 1807, when the Portuguese royal family fled the country for Brazil in the face of Napoleon's advancing army, it was still incomplete, and it was not finished until the later nineteenth century. By then, Portugal's imperial glory was fading, and in the 5 October 1910 Revolution its royal family was overthrown and a republic established. However, Belém remained as a symbol of Portugal's golden age, and in 1983 its Tower and the Monastery of Jerónimos were designated UNESCO World Heritage Sites.

CAPE COAST CASTLE

. . . .

The transatlantic slave trade is one of the great tragedies of history. From the sixteenth to nineteenth century, over 12 million African people were enslaved and transported to the Americas. European powers established outposts across the West African coast, one of which was Cape Coast Castle, in modern-day Ghana.

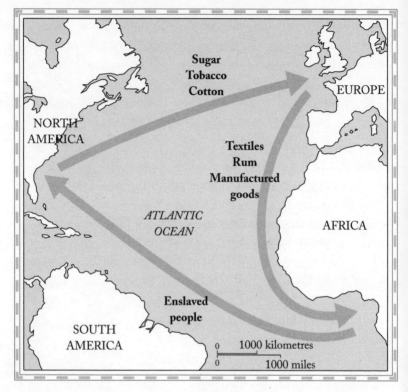

Sugar
Tobacco
Cotton

EUROPE

NORTH AMERICA

Textiles
Rum
Manufactured
goods

ATLANTIC OCEAN

AFRICA

Enslaved people

SOUTH AMERICA

| 0 | 1000 kilometres |
| 0 | 1000 miles |

The Triangular Trade in the eighteenth century

The first European slave traders to operate in West Africa were the Portuguese, who established themselves there during the mid-fifteenth century. By the early sixteenth century, they had been joined by the Spanish, British, French and Dutch. The main destination for enslaved people was the Americas; about half of the people enslaved in Africa were sent to the Caribbean, a third to Brazil, and most of the remainder to North America.

THE OLD POLO GROUNDS, ACCRA

By the mid-twentieth century, there was gathering opposition to European colonial rule across Africa. In the British colony of the Gold Coast, the leading light in the struggle for self-government was Kwame Nkrumah (1909–72). On 6 March 1957, just after midnight, he addressed a huge crowd gathered at the Old Polo Grounds in Accra and proclaimed the independence of Ghana (named after the African medieval empire). As Ghana was the first sub-Saharan British colony to become independent, it became an iconic and epochal event.

By the seventeenth century, these Europeans had established a 'triangular trade', in which ships carried manufactured goods to Africa, purchased slaves there to transport to the Americas, and then returned home carrying raw materials such as tobacco, sugar or cotton. The section between Africa and the Americas was known as the Middle Passage. Conditions on the ships that sailed the route were cramped, inhumane and disease-ridden; many threw themselves overboard. Perhaps 15 per cent of the people who were enslaved died on the Middle Passage.

One of the regions of West Africa where Europeans were most active became known as the Gold Coast (it, and nearby areas such as the Ivory Coast and the Slave Coast, were named after their main export). Although there were rich deposits of gold there that Europeans sought to exploit, they were also eager to carry on their trade in human lives there as well. On a stretch of coast less than 482 km (300 miles) long, over sixty trading posts, lodges and forts were built by European merchants, which they used to hold people before they were loaded on ships to make the Middle Passage.

The history of Cape Coast Castle goes back to the mid-seventeenth century, and Hendrik Carloff, who probably came from the Baltic trading city of Rostock (although he may also have been born in Finland), and had worked for the Dutch West India Company in West Africa, where he forged connections with several local rulers. They included King Bodema of Efutu, who ruled an area of coastline in modern-day Ghana. In 1648, Carloff returned to Europe, where he made contact with the De Geers, a family of Walloon origin who had emigrated to Sweden and made a fortune in iron manufacture. The De Geers were founders of the Swedish Africa Company and contracted Carloff as a director. In 1650, he sailed back to the Gold Coast, where he re-established relations with Bodema and gained permission to build a lodge on a piece of land the Portuguese had named Cabo Corço, which was corrupted into English as Cape Coast. A square structure of timber and mud bricks was constructed in 1653 and named Carolusburg in honour of Charles X Gustav of Sweden (1622–60). Carloff left for Europe in 1655 but soon fell out with the De Geers. He then began working for the

Danish, who wanted to establish themselves in the slave trade. In 1658, this time working for the Danish Africa Company, Carloff travelled back to the Gold Coast, where he persuaded Bodema's advisors to transfer Carolusburg to the Danish. Backed up by armed ships, he gained control of the fort, before returning to Europe. This ends Carloff's involvement with the Gold Coast, although he later worked for the French West India Company in West Africa and the Caribbean.

Danish control of Carolusburg did not last long. In 1659, the Dutch captured it, before Sweden resumed possession the year after. However, the Swedish were unable to make any profits from the site, and so handed it back to the Dutch in 1663. On 7 May 1664, an English fleet took the fort, which had fallen into disrepair. Renamed Cape Coast Castle, it became the headquarters for the British involvement in the transatlantic slave trade. During the 1680s and 1690s, the Fort underwent significant renovations; its north side was extended and a new building jutting out over the sea was constructed as a platform for cannons. At first the British continued to pay monthly rent to the King of Efutu, before transferring it to the leaders of the Fante, an alliance of states that absorbed its territory.

After the mid-eighteenth century, increased demand for enslaved labour in the Americas meant that European slave traders increased their activity in West Africa. Consequently, the transatlantic slave trade peaked during the 1780s, when around 88,000 slaves were transported every year. Around this time the last vestiges of the old, by now dilapidated, fort were demolished, to make way for a larger building. The new Cape Coast Castle had a tower, double bastion and ramps that extended all the way to the beach, making landing supplies easier. It also had extensive underground vaults that could hold hundreds of slaves, who were kept there until ships came to purchase them. Cape Coast Castle became a valued destination for slave-ship captains because they could quickly load their ships to capacity, and so minimize time spent anchored on the coast.

In 1807, the slave trade was abolished in the British Empire, but they did not abandon Cape Coast Castle, hoping to use it as a base for plantations in the surrounding countryside. By this time, the Fante Confederacy was being challenged for local dominance by the Kingdom of Ashanti, to whom the British paid rent for Cape Coast Castle from 1817. The British soon found themselves challenged by the Ashanti, who, in 1825, gathered a large army to try to capture Cape Coast Castle, but an outbreak of smallpox forced them to withdraw. In 1867, the British formally established the colony of Gold Coast, and continued to fight the Ashanti and the Fante as they pushed into the interior. Cape Coast Castle remained, and after Ghanaian independence was established in 1957 it was, along with other slave castles, restored and preserved to bear witness to the horrors that had occurred there.

GREENWICH

· · · · · · · · · · · · · · · · · ·

British history, particularly of its empire, is inextricably bound up with the seas. Few places in the nation have a greater maritime legacy than Greenwich.

Greenwich became associated with the English royal family during the thirteenth century, when the area was used by them as a hunting park. It became a royal residence in 1447, when the Crown took ownership of a manor house that became known as the Palace of Placentia, which was built on the Thames in an area of parkland. As it was close to London, Henry VII (1457–1509), the first monarch of the Tudor dynasty, selected it as his principal residence, and rebuilt it. It was the birthplace of his son and successor, Henry VIII (1491–1547), who often hosted banquets and jousts at Placentia. His daughter Elizabeth I (1533–1603) was also born there, and used it as a summer residence.

The Stuart monarchs James I (1566–1625) and Charles I (1600–49) were also frequent visitors to Greenwich. In 1613, James I granted the manor and palace to his wife, Anna of Denmark (1574–1619), by way of an apology after he had furiously overreacted to her accidentally shooting his favourite dog while they were out hunting. She decided to build her own residence near to Placentia, and the architect Inigo Jones (1573–1652) received the commission to design the 'Queen's House' in 1616, with work beginning the next year. Reflecting the architectural trends of continental Europe, it was Britain's first-ever classically inspired building. By the time it had been completed in 1635, Anna had died. By then, her son Charles I was on the throne, and the Queen's House was given to his wife, Henrietta Maria of France (1609–69).

From 1639 to 1651, England, Wales, Scotland and Ireland descended into a series of civil wars between the Crown and Parliament. During the conflict, Charles I was tried for placing his own interests above his people's, found guilty of high treason and executed. The Parliamentarians, led by Oliver Cromwell (1599–1658), ultimately triumphed and a republican Commonwealth was established. Placentia fell into disrepair – Cromwell tried to sell it, and when he could not, had it first turned into a factory making biscuits for the navy, then used to hold prisoners of war.

BOUVINES

Following the Norman Conquest of 1066, English monarchs held lands across the Channel, often creating conflict with France – notably, the Hundred Years' War (1337–1453). An earlier Anglo-French war occurred in 1213–14. The final battle was at Bouvines in northern France, where the English and their allies were roundly defeated. King John (1166–1216) was left so weakened that in 1215 he submitted to his barons' demand for the Magna Carta, a charter limiting royal power. This helped create common law in England, guaranteeing individual rights.

Particularly after Cromwell's death in 1658, finding a permanent political settlement proved difficult and led to the Restoration of the monarchy under Charles II (1630–85) in 1660. He had Placentia torn down, and ordered a new palace be built there. Due to lack of funds, it was never finished, although Charles II did remodel Greenwich Park in the latest style imported from France. His greatest legacy to Greenwich was commissioning the Royal Observatory, which was designed by Sir Christopher Wren (1632–1723), the architect instrumental in the rebuilding of London after the Great Fire of 1666. Situated on a hill in Greenwich Park, the

Royal Observatory was built for the first Astronomer Royal, John Flamsteed (1646–1719), who moved there in 1676. Its location outside London meant there was no smoke to obscure his work scanning the skies. The observatory's research was hugely beneficial to mariners in their navigation. Its *Nautical Almanac* was used by mariners from across the world. As it set Greenwich's longitude as the reference point for time and location in its calculations and charts, in 1884 the location became the international standard for the 'prime meridian' – the line defined as 0° longitude. It is also the baseline for the global time zone system.

In 1688, James II (1633–1701), who had converted to Catholicism, was overthrown in the Glorious Revolution and replaced by his daughter Mary II (1662–94) and her Dutch husband, William of Orange (1650–1702). As part of their ascension they agreed to the Bill of Rights (1689), which guaranteed the rights of Parliament and laid the foundation for its supremacy over the Crown. With residences at Hampton Court and Kensington, the Crown had no need or desire to complete the rebuilding at Greenwich. Instead, in 1694, Mary II declared the site would be used to house retired sailors and gave Wren the task of designing Greenwich Hospital. He delivered a Baroque masterpiece (partly financed by fines on merchants for smuggling) that was completed in 1742. Also in the complex was the Royal Hospital School, founded for the orphans of sailors. From 1806, it was largely moved to the Queen's House, which had two new wings added. Greenwich Hospital was closed in 1869, and from 1873 was the home of the Royal Naval College, providing training for its officers. In 1933, the Royal Hospital School moved to Suffolk, and four years later the Queen's House was reopened to the public as part of the National Maritime Museum. Meanwhile, Greenwich ceased to be the residence of the Astronomer Royal in 1948. By 1957, its official function had ended (pollution meant observations could no longer be made there, so that function was moved to Sussex), and it was converted into a museum. In 1998, the Royal Navy left Greenwich; the college's magnificent buildings are now open to the public, and also used by the University of Greenwich and Trinity College of Music.

Although naval strength and scientific innovation were important components of the British Empire that grew up over the seventeenth, eighteenth and nineteenth century, economic factors were what truly shaped it. Fittingly, just a few metres from the Old Royal Naval College is a monument to Britain's past as the world's greatest trading power: the *Cutty Sark*, a clipper launched in Dumbarton, Scotland, in 1869. It made its maiden voyage in 1870, sailing to Shanghai via the Cape of Good Hope on the lucrative tea run. However, the opening of the Suez Canal meant this route was no longer used, so the ship was employed to carry wool from Australia to Britain. After steam supplanted sail power, the *Cutty Sark* was used as a training ship, until in 1957 it was fully restored and placed in a concrete dry dock. It is a living reminder that, ultimately, commercial considerations were what primarily contributed to the growth and continuation of British imperialism.

CAPE TRAFALGAR

Maritime power was the foundation of the British Empire, allowing the control of important sea routes and defending the home country from invasion. Perhaps the Royal Navy's greatest victory was achieved off Cape Trafalgar, in south-west Spain. On 27 September 1805, Horatio Nelson (1758–1805), who died in the battle, led the Royal Navy to victory over a Franco-Spanish fleet. Consequently, Britain dominated the seas for the rest of the Napoleonic Wars, a mastery that continued throughout the nineteenth century.

THE HALL OF MIRRORS
AT VERSAILLES PALACE

No monarch embodied absolute royal power more than Louis XIV (1638–1715) of France, the 'Sun King' who reigned for over seventy-two years. The site that symbolized his majesty was Versailles, which he built into the grandest palace in Europe.

Louis XIV came to the throne in 1643, after the death of his father, Louis XIII (1601–43). He was just four years old, which contributed to the political instability that struck France during the mid-seventeenth century. From 1648 to 1653, the country was embroiled in the Fronde civil wars between supporters and opponents of the centralization of royal authority. The Royalists would triumph, contributing to the emergence of absolutism. As Louis XIV was a minor, the Italian-born Cardinal Jules Mazarin (1602–61) acted as regent, but after he died in 1661 the young king assumed personal rule, continuing Mazarin's centralizing policies, and transforming France into Europe's greatest power.

For the first part of his reign, Louis XIV travelled between different royal chateaux as well as the royal palaces in Paris, the Louvre and Tuileries. One of his aims was to build a great palace for his Bourbon dynasty, which had only ruled France since 1589. There was nowhere in Paris large enough to satisfy his ambitions, and the city was congested and had water-supply problems. Seeking a blank slate, Louis XIV turned to the countryside, and a small hunting lodge his father had built in Versailles, 16 km (10 miles) from Paris. He would use it as the basis for his own palace. It would be entirely his creation, and reflect how he wanted to express himself to his kingdom and subjects. Work began in 1661, and would continue in several phases until 1710 (Louis XIV's successors would later add to it).

The construction of Versailles was an ongoing effort, and required a workforce of up to 20,000 – many of them died as a result of malarial fever because of the swampy ground. In addition to the palace, elaborate formal gardens were added with fountains, artificial lakes, manicured trees and statues. One of the great difficulties was ensuring the water supply was sufficient, and underneath its grounds are endless pipes and vaults. When its building was at its peak, Versailles accounted for about 4 per cent of France's total state budget.

The royal family began to spend more time in Versailles after 1674 and moved there in 1678. The court was officially established there in 1682. The grounds of Versailles were always open – anyone who was dressed appropriately was permitted to enter and explore the gardens (men had to wear swords – these could be rented at the gates). Access to the palace itself, and the royal presence, was harder to gain, and required some kind of inside knowledge. Those who were allowed to venture inside were met with an elaborate spectacle; throughout the palace, the motif of the Sun appeared repeatedly, showing that Louis XIV expected his courtiers and people to revolve around him. The Greek god Apollo was another recurring feature of the decoration. There was also ample space for fetes and shows, and Louis XIV would often perform in ballets himself, appearing in elaborate costumes, as the Sun or a Roman emperor. One of the most beautiful rooms in the palace was the Hall of Mirrors, built between 1678 and 1689. It was over 70 m (230 feet) long and had seventeen mirrors (then incredibly expensive to produce) facing the same number of windows overlooking the garden. On the ceiling were chandeliers and images of Louis XIV's early reign, while the marble walls were decorated with statues and reliefs. By the time Louis XIV died in 1715, Versailles was the size of a small town, with over 25,000 residents. All senior government offices were based there, and all nobles were expected to spend time there every year.

Louis XIV was succeeded by his great-grandson Louis XV (1710–74) under whom royal absolutism declined; by then France no longer dominated Europe, facing challenges from other great powers, particularly Britain. When Louis XVI (1754–93) came to the throne in 1774, government finances were in a parlous state, made worse by his decision to formally enter the American Revolutionary War in 1778. Although France helped the rebels defeat the British, it contributed to financial crisis, and the Crown suspending payments to its debtors in 1788. To try to address this problem, Louis XVI called the Estates General, a national advisory body. It gathered at Versailles on 5 May 1789. Neither the king nor the 1,200 delegates realized the meeting would sow the seeds of revolution.

PLACE DE LA CONCORDE, PARIS

On 21 January 1793, Louis XVI was guillotined after being found guilty of high treason. The execution took place on the Place de la Révolution (previously named for Louis XV), the largest public square in Paris. Several other high-profile figures were also guillotined there, including Louis's wife Marie Antoinette (1755–93) and Maximilien Robespierre (1758–94). In 1795, as a sign of the desire to bring together the nation after the bloodshed and turmoil of the Revolution, the square was renamed Place de la Concorde.

Louis XVI clashed with the Third Estate, the Commons, and closed the hall where they were meeting. Instead, on 20 June, they gathered in a tennis court, vowing they would not dissolve until a constitution was established. Louis XVI was forced to recognize their validity. The first and second estates joined the third to form a National Constituent Assembly. Louis XVI had lost control. From then on, the Crown's authority was in decline. That October, in the midst of food shortages and high prices, a crowd from Paris (most of whom were women) marched on Versailles. They forced the royal family to move to the Tuileries in Paris. From 1789 to 1793, the revolutionary government became more radical; France was declared a republic and the king, suspected of colluding with hostile foreign powers, was executed.

France faced war with its neighbours (as well as internal conflict) but survived. Following the Reign of Terror (1793–4), in which thousands of 'enemies of the Revolution' were purged, a more conservative regime, the Directory, took power in 1795. It was always weak, and in 1799 a young general called Napoleon Bonaparte (1769–1821) overthrew it, and crowned himself Emperor in 1804. For most of the Revolutionary and Napoleonic years, Versailles was largely abandoned. It was restored during the mid-nineteenth century, and used as a museum and for government functions. During the Franco-Prussian War (1870–1), which saw France roundly defeated, it served as the headquarters of the German forces besieging Paris. As a result of the victory, Wilhelm I (1797–1888) was declared Emperor of a unified Germany – a title officially proclaimed in the Hall of Mirrors on 18 January 1871.

The German Empire would not last half a century; on 9 November 1918, facing defeat in the First World War and with his country in turmoil, Wilhelm I's grandson Wilhelm II (1859–1941) abdicated. Two days later the Great War was over. Peace talks took place the next year in Paris, with the victorious powers unilaterally deciding its terms. The resulting Treaty of Versailles, signed on 28 June 1919 in the Hall of Mirrors, imposed harsh terms on Germany such as territorial losses, reparations, disarmament and forcing it to admit to its guilt in starting the conflict. The Treaty's severity was one of the contributing factors to the Nazi rise to power in Germany during the 1930s, and the eventual outbreak of the Second World War. Versailles, increasingly used solely as a tourist attraction, survived this next conflict intact, and since 2003 has been the subject of an extensive renovation programme.

THE PLAINS OF ABRAHAM

. . . .

The Seven Years' War (1756–63) was the first global conflict. In North America, it saw Britain defeat France, with its capture of Quebec in 1759 proving instrumental. This was achieved thanks to a battle fought outside the city, in an area of fields known as the Plains of Abraham.

France and Britain had been vying for imperial dominance over North American since the later seventeenth century. 'New France' (comprising the two colonies of Canada and Louisiana, which covered a great swathe of the centre and north of the continent) was geographically larger than Britain's Thirteen Colonies, which were located along the Atlantic seaboard. However, the population of the British colonies – about 2 million – was greater than France's, which had a population of around 70,000.

When Britain declared war on France in May 1756, the two countries' colonists, together with their Native American allies, had already been fighting for two years. At first, the French won several victories. The arrival of British regulars, who reinforced the American militia, and the Royal Navy's ability to intercept

French ships carrying reinforcements and supplies, would prove crucial in turning the tide of the war. By 1759 the British could call on 50,000 men, while the French had only 15,000. That year, the British launched an attack into Canada. One of their main targets was the formidable fortress-city of Quebec, which sat on the high ground overlooking the north bank of the Saint Lawrence River.

Leading the Quebec expedition was James Wolfe (1727–59). He was just thirty-two; a highly ambitious man who had lobbied in London to be given the job, which was his first independent command. Wolfe landed his 8,600 troops on 26 June at the Île d'Orléans, an island in the Saint Lawrence River east of Quebec. Four days later, he crossed the river to seize Point Levi, which lay on the riverbank opposite Quebec, allowing him to mount batteries that could fire on the city. Despite heavy shelling and several forays, he was unable to make a breakthrough. Commanding the French army was Louis-Joseph de Montcalm (1712–59), a somewhat arrogant nobleman. He looked with disdain upon the local militia, relegating them to guard or support duties, and refused to let them train alongside his regulars. Although he was able to see off the initial British attack, he was running low on supplies and was outnumbered.

By September, the siege was still dragging on. Wolfe was in ill health due to kidney stones and to a fever that had left a third of his men unfit for duty. He began to clash with his officer staff, who demanded he mount a direct assault on Quebec. Accordingly, early on 13 September, Wolfe landed with around

4,800 men at Anse au Foulon, a spot at the foot of a cliff 3.2 km (2 miles) from Quebec's western walls. With British ships providing a diversion further upriver, the British forces climbed up the 53-metre-high (175-foot) cliff, and shortly after the break of dawn were marching across the Plains of Abraham.

ALBANY CITY HALL

From 19 June to 11 July 1754, delegates from seven of the thirteen British colonies in North America gathered in upstate New York at Albany City Hall. They discussed measures to defend themselves against the French and alliances with the tribes of the Iroquois Confederacy. Although Benjamin Franklin's (1706–90) plan proposing the unification of the government of the Thirteen Colonies was rejected, the Albany Congress sowed the seeds of their later association during the revolution against British rule.

Montcalm rushed 4,000 troops to meet them without waiting for reinforcements. Short of men, he had intermingled relatively inexperienced local militia with his regulars. Battle was joined at 10 a.m. The French forces' lack of coordination meant they fired on the British line too soon. The British forces held steady, and waited until their enemy had closed to within 37 metres (40 yards). They then launched a disciplined and devastating volley of musket fire. The French lines broke, and they retreated. Within half an hour the battle was won. As Wolfe was urging his men on, he was shot through the intestines and chest. The wound was fatal, but he retained consciousness long enough to hear that the French had been defeated. While Montcalm was riding back to Quebec, he was shot in the back and died the next day.

With their commander-in-chief dead, the British dug in rather than mount an assault on Quebec. The superiority of their position meant that on 18 September Quebec surrendered to the British. The next April, the French attempted to retake Quebec. Although they won a battle, also fought on the Plains of Abraham, the British were able to retreat behind the city walls. The French did not have the firepower to take Quebec and were forced to withdraw on 15 May when news came that British reinforcements were arriving. That September, the British captured Montreal, the last major city in French hands.

The Seven Years' War ended in 1763. Under the Treaty of Paris, France gave up Canada to Britain, while Louisiana was handed over to Spain (which ceded Florida to the British). The only French territory remaining was the tiny islands of Saint Pierre and Miquelon, just off the shore of Newfoundland, which they were allowed to retain as a refuge for their fishermen, so they could continue to ply the coasts of Newfoundland. Today, the islands are a semi-autonomous French territory. After over a century under British rule, in 1867, the provinces of Canada federated as a dominion with domestic self-government, and became independent in 1931. The French influence remained strong, and the country is officially bilingual. The Plains of Abraham are now a public park in Quebec.

Although the British had been victorious, the costs of the war had been a high burden for the government to bear, as was continuing to defend the frontiers of the Thirteen Colonies after the fighting ended. When the British government attempted to impose taxation on their American colonies to pay for their military expenses, it would contribute to anger among the local population, precipitating the eventual outbreak of the American War of Independence in 1775.

7

THE AGE OF REVOLUTIONS

BOIS CAÏMAN

The transatlantic slave trade saw millions of people enslaved and sent to the Americas. There was widespread resistance, such as sabotage or escape. Furthermore, there were frequent uprisings of enslaved people – none was larger or more successful than the one that occurred in Saint-Domingue, later known as Haiti.

Hispaniola, after Cuba, is the second-largest island in the West Indies. Its western side had been a French colony known as Saint-Domingue since they conquered it from Spain (who maintained control of the eastern side, San Domingo) in the mid-seventeenth century. Saint-Domingue became France's most lucrative colony, thanks to the slaves who worked on its sugar, coffee, cotton, indigo and cocoa plantations. By the later eighteenth century, there were around 500,000 people enslaved there, with a population of around 40,000 Europeans (as well as some free black people, often employed for patrol and militia duties). Conditions on the plantations were among the harshest in the Caribbean, and brutal punishments were used. During the later eighteenth and early nineteenth century, Saint-Domingue was caught up in the conflict that swept through Europe as a result of the French Revolution. With revolutionary concepts of liberty and freedom ringing through France, in 1790 the National Assembly had granted full civil rights to free black men who owned property and whose parents had both been free. This measure was opposed by many whites in Saint-Domingue, and created significant tensions along racial and ideological lines.

On the night of 21/2 August 1791, a mass slave revolt broke out in the north of Saint-Domingue, which would eventually transform the balance of power in the colony. It had been organized in secret by a group of slaves from various plantations in the area. The recent political upheaval had allowed them to plan undisturbed. They had made their plans one week before the insurrection, meeting in the middle of the night in an area of forest called Bois Caïman. As part of the meeting they had staged a voodoo ceremony, sacrificing a black pig. By the end of August, over 1,000 plantations had been burned down (the sugarcane fields were particularly flammable) and around 2,000 Europeans killed. Although the revolt was mostly contained in the northern plains of Saint-Domingue, it was already the largest the Caribbean had ever seen. In 1792, the French revolutionary leader Léger-Félicité Sonthonax (1763–1813) arrived with 7,000 soldiers to maintain control of Saint-Domingue. Under his command, government forces regained control, and drove the revolt leaders to camps in the mountains. Despite this setback, the uprising that had been planned at Bois Caïman would be the catalyst for a much wider uprising that would have lasting repercussions for Saint-Domingue.

One of the revolt leaders was Toussaint Bréda (1743–1803). He had been born into slavery, but won manumission at around the age of twenty-five. An educated man, he eventually owned his own plantation (as well as some slaves). He decided to join the revolt, adopting a new surname, Louverture ('The Opening'), to signify that he intended to bring liberty to Saint-Domingue. Louverture took control of the insurgent army and continued to fight against the French. He was supported by the Spanish, one of the many European powers seeking to overthrow France's revolutionary regime. In May 1794, the French government formally abolished slavery. After hearing the news, Louverture swung his support behind France. By 1795, Spain would make peace with the French, and cede control of all Hispaniola to them. British forces invaded Saint-Domingue in 1797 – Louverture was given command of the forces charged with resisting them, and forced them to withdraw by 1798. He then spent the next three years consolidating control of Saint-Domingue, defeating domestic rivals.

PALMARES

From the sixteenth to nineteenth century, more enslaved people from Africa were sent to Brazil than to any other place. Thousands of slaves escaped plantations to form their own communities, known as quilombos. From 1605, several quilombos in north-eastern Brazil joined together into a single community, called Palmares. By the end of the seventeenth century it had a population of over 20,000, ruled by an elected chief. Palmares fought off a series of Portuguese attempts to subdue it until it was finally defeated in 1694. Slavery would persist in Brazil until 1888.

With his authority unquestioned, in 1801, Louverture issued a constitution for Saint-Domingue – it called for its autonomy, popular sovereignty, equality under the law for all and permanent abolition of slavery, as well as naming him governor for life. This display of power was too much for France's new master, Napoleon, who dispatched his brother-in-law Charles Leclerc (1772–1802) to Saint-Domingue with over 10,000 troops to regain control of the colony and also restore slavery. After the French expedition landed in February 1802, Louverture realized their numbers were so great that he could not defeat them and so retreated into the mountainous interior. The fighting went badly for him, and within three months many of his generals were surrendering. That May, with his position untenable, Louverture gave himself up to the French in exchange for a pardon and their assurances he would be left in peace. They reneged on the promise, arresting him and taking him to France, where he was imprisoned in a chateau in the Jura Mountains. He died there on 7 April 1803.

With Louverture gone, his lieutenant Jean-Jacques Dessalines (1758–1806) took control of the forces that continued to fight the French, whose numbers were rapidly declining because of tropical diseases like yellow fever (which killed Leclerc in November 1802). Even so, the bitter fighting continued and the death toll mounted. On 30 November 1803, the French finally surrendered to Dessalines. On 1 January 1804, he proclaimed independence for Haiti, adopting the indigenous Arawak name for the island as a symbol of its break from European control, and establishing the first black republic in the world. France would not formally recognize Haitian independence until 1825, and only did so in return for a huge indemnity that crippled the finances of the nascent state that had already been unsettled by years of bloodshed. Haiti continued to struggle to find prosperity and stability, and was frequently blighted by natural disaster and civil strife; even so, it occupies a leading place in the annals of freedom as the only place where slaves were able to cast off their shackles and permanently establish an independent nation for themselves.

CLAPHAM

During the eighteenth and nineteenth century, the abolitionist movement became a global campaign against slavery. One of the most influential groups were the Clapham Sect, a group of Christians who were involved in a wide range of social reforms and met in the London suburb of Clapham. One of their most prominent members was William Wilberforce (1759–1833), who helped secure the legislation that banned the slave trade in the British Empire in 1807 and abolished it (with some exceptions) in 1833.

WILHELMSTRASSE

. . . .

Berlin has played a major role in world, and European, history; having been the centre of Prussian, then German, power. From the later nineteenth century, Wilhelmstrasse housed the most important official buildings, before long a synonym for the state's government.

Berlin was founded in the early thirteenth century, becoming part of Brandenburg, a state of the Holy Roman Empire (a patchwork of different territories that covered modern-day Germany and parts of surrounding countries) located in what is now eastern Germany and western Poland. In 1411, Brandenburg came under the rule of the Hohenzollern family, who made Berlin their capital. During the mid-sixteenth century, like many other German rulers, they converted to Lutheranism. The Hohenzollerns of Brandenburg increased their territory after inheriting the crown of Prussia, a state to the east, in 1618.

By the early eighteenth century, Berlin had become a major city. Under Frederick William I (1688–1740) new streets were laid out, including the Husarenstrasse, which after his death was renamed Wilhelmstrasse in his honour. The man who turned Prussia into the leading power in Germany was Frederick II – 'the Great' – (1712–86), a military genius whose forty-six-year reign saw steady territorial growth. A son of the Enlightenment, he was also a great patron of arts and learning, building an opera house, library and scientific academy in Berlin.

During the nineteenth century, Berlin, like the rest of Prussia, embraced industrialization and grew into one of Europe's great manufacturing centres. Wilhelmstrasse, previously a wealthy residential area, became the centre of the Prussian government. In 1871, Wilhelm I of Prussia (1797–1888) became Kaiser of the German Empire, uniting the various German states under his rule. The architect of this process was the Prussian statesman Otto von Bismarck (1815–98), who became the first Chancellor of the German Empire. He established his office in a Rococo-style noble residence on Wilhelmstrasse (the Foreign Office was housed next door). The Reich Chancellery hosted numerous international meetings, including the 1878 Congress of Berlin, where Europe's great powers met to redraw the map of the Balkans and establish independent nations there in the light of declining Ottoman power. In 1884–5, the Berlin Conference was held in the Reich Chancellery, where thirteen European nations (and the United States) unilaterally set out how they would carve up African territory among themselves.

The German Empire fell apart in 1918, as a result of its impending defeat in the First World War. On 9 November of that year, the final kaiser, Wilhelm II (1859–1941), abdicated, and Germany became a democratic parliamentary republic. Although Berlin was officially the capital, fighting in the city meant its constitution was decided in the city of Weimar. This Weimar Republic struggled with political discord and economic problems. In 1933, Adolf Hitler (1889–1945), leader of the fascist Nazi Party, became its chancellor at the head of a coalition government. Hitler and the Nazis then seized total control, making themselves the only legal party and violently persecuting political opponents and Germany's Jewish population.

WARTBURG CASTLE

Overlooking the town of Eisenach, Wartburg Castle dates back to the mid-eleventh century and by 1485 had come under the rule of the Dukes of Saxony. Wartburg played a central role in the life of Martin Luther (1483–1546), who in 1521 had been excommunicated and outlawed for his criticisms of the Catholic Church. Frederick III of Saxony (1463–1525), who believed Luther had been treated unfairly, sheltered him at Wartburg for nearly a year. There Luther began his German translation of the New Testament and wrote numerous religious tracts. He would then go on to play a pivotal role in sparking the Protestant Reformation.

Hitler wished to make Berlin an imperial capital, befitting his expansionist plans for the Third Reich. He found the Old Reich Chancellery too undistinguished, and commissioned his favourite architect, Albert Speer (1905–81), to design a new building for the headquarters of his government. It was finished in 1938, and projected the stern authoritarianism of Nazism (nearby was another new addition to the Wilhelmstrasse, the Ministry of Aviation). One of the most important locations on Wilhelmstrasse lay beneath it: the Führerbunker. Begun in 1936 and wholly rebuilt in 1944, it was part of an extensive underground complex for the officials and politicians who ran Germany. Hitler's personal bunker was over 9 m (30 feet) below ground, and encased in 3 m (10 feet) of concrete covered by granite slabs and steel mesh, meaning it could survive even a direct hit. Entry to the bunker was via a spiral staircase blocked by huge steel doors and guarded by men from the Leibstandarte SS Adolf Hitler, the Führer's personal bodyguard. The Führerbunker itself had eighteen cramped rooms, was 557 square m (6,000 square feet) in size, and had its own generator and pump room to keep it supplied with power and water. The ventilation system was incredibly noisy, but when turned off the bunker became unbearably hot.

By 1945, the Allied powers were closing in on Germany from both sides. With defeat inevitable, Hitler retreated to his bunker, becoming virtually a permanent resident. His final public appearance outside it was on 20 April, to award medals to boy recruits commended for their futile attempts to stave off the Soviet advance. By then, Berlin was in ruins, pounded to rubble by Allied bombers and the artillery of the advancing Soviets. On 30 April, unwilling to be captured alive, Hitler committed suicide in the bunker. The German surrender came on 8 May, ending the Second World War in Europe. The Battle of Berlin resulted in 304,000 Soviet casualties, while German military losses may have been over 1 million. At least 100,000 civilians were killed in the fighting. The buildings of Wilhelmstrasse lay in ruins; after the war many of those not obliterated were demolished to prevent them from becoming shrines for Nazi sympathizers.

After the war, Berlin, like Germany, was divided. West Berlin, which had been the American, British and French occupation zone, became an enclave within the communist state of East Germany. Symbolic of this was the Berlin Wall, built in 1961 by the East German authorities, which divided Wilhelmstrasse. Much of the thoroughfare was in East Berlin, where the authorities did not wish to build government offices on a street so synonymous with fascism, meaning Wilhelmstrasse lost much of its former status. Berlin, and Wilhelmstrasse, was only rejoined in 1989, when the Wall fell as part of the continent-wide collapse of communist regimes; the following year, East and West Germany were formally reunited.

NEW LANARK MILLS

. . . .

The Industrial Revolution transformed manufacturing, and fundamentally altered societies and economies across the world. This began in eighteenth-century Britain, where the first true factories were built. One of the earliest was New Lanark Mills in Scotland.

The first modern factory was Cromford Mill in Derbyshire, established in 1771. As with much innovation in the mechanization of production during this era, it was focused on textile manufacturing. Its founder was Richard Arkwright (1732–92), a former wig-maker who had invented the water frame, a machine that produced strong cotton thread. As it was powered by a water-wheel, it was unsuitable for domestic manufacture, so had to be placed in a factory. Arkwright became hugely successful, employing hundreds of workers and opening a second mill nearby five years later. Over the rest of the eighteenth and nineteenth century, the production of textiles was fully mechanized and largely relocated to factories; a pattern repeated in many other industries. This was accompanied by huge advances in productivity, as well as a shift of the population from rural areas to towns and cities.

In 1783, Arkwright was invited by David Dale (1739–1806), a Scottish entrepreneur, to survey the site of a potential new factory near the town of Lanark, on the banks of the River Clyde. Together with the banker George Dempster (1732–1818) they formed a partnership, and within the year work had begun on a plot of land they called New Lanark. It was situated at a spot where the Clyde ran through a narrow gorge, meaning the water could drive wheels that would spin raw cotton into thread (the water supply was regulated by building a dam, tunnels and channels). Dale dissolved the partnership in 1785 and continued as sole proprietor; the first mill at New Lanark went into operation in 1786 and a second was begun in 1788. By 1793, there were over 1,100 people working at New Lanark, which had become a thriving planned community. Initially, only a third of its residents were adults; as was common in eighteenth-century factories, child and teen labour was used (many were orphans from Glasgow or Edinburgh, or migrants from the Highlands). The working day began at 6 a.m. and lasted until 7 p.m., however, children were given two hours of teaching per day.

New Lanark attracted many visitors; including Robert Owen (1771–1858), a Welsh-born businessman who in 1798 was running a successful cotton mill in Manchester. While in Scotland, Owen fell in love with Dale's daughter Caroline, and they married in 1799. Owen then headed a partnership that purchased New Lanark from his father-in-law for £60,000 and took over management on New Year's Day 1800. He increased the working day to fourteen hours. Above each person's workplace was a piece of wood called the 'monitor' – each side was differently coloured to display the conduct of the worker the day before (black for bad, blue for indifferent, yellow for good and white for excellent). These were noted in 'books of character' that monitored performance over time. Owen took steps to improve life for the people of New Lanark, where housing conditions were previously poor. He employed watchmen to patrol the streets for drunkenness, established a sick fund for workers and a village shop that sold goods at virtually cost price.

Although business at New Lanark continued to boom, some of Owen's partners believed he should prioritize profit and abandon his plans to improve the lives of his employees. This approach was prevalent in the majority of the factories that had sprung

SWIFT & COMPANY'S MEAT-PACKING HOUSE, CHICAGO, ILLINOIS

Modern mass production relies on the moving assembly line. From the nineteenth century, factories began to be built so that manufacturing was carried out sequentially, with each workstation adding a new component. A famed symbol of this mode of production is the Ford factory in Highland Park, Michigan, which from 1913 could build a Model T in just 150 minutes. Its designers were inspired by visiting a slaughterhouse in Chicago, where a conveyor system moved animal carcasses down a line to be butchered, with each worker removing the same cut.

up across Europe and North America, where conditions were often dangerous, unhygienic and harsh. In 1813, Owen re-established the business, taking on investors who agreed with his approach. Owen would eventually cut the working day to eight hours, and in 1816 opened the New Institution for the Formation of Character in the central square at New Lanark. This was a school that children entered at eighteen months, remaining there until at least the age of ten. In addition to an elementary education, they were also taught singing and dancing; the building remained open in the evenings for older children and teenagers to take classes. Social reformers and educators flocked to New Lanark – even the future Emperor Nicholas I of Russia (1796–1855) paid a visit.

From 1817, Owen began to make ambitious proposals for social reform. Using New Lanark as a model, he proposed self-contained communities of 1,200 where the inhabitants would live, work and raise families communally. Enlarging on this, he foresaw a socialistic society based on cooperation and the pursuit of the common good. To put his plans into action, Owen migrated to the United States in 1824, selling New Lanark the year after. He purchased land in Indiana and established the community of New Harmony. His utopian plans floundered under the stress of internal disputes, and Owen left in 1827, having lost £40,000 (80 per cent of his fortune). Although Owenite communities sprang up across the United States, Canada, Ireland and Britain, none lasted. Owen returned to his homeland, where he campaigned for social reform and trade unionism before his death in 1858.

New Lanark continued to operate. The more and more efficient steam engines pioneered by James Watt (1736–1819) and Matthew Boulton (1728–1809) had made it less necessary to base factories on riverside sites that could make use of water-wheels. Indeed, the energy output of steam engines soon outweighed the water-wheel. By the 1880s, steam power was introduced to New Lanark, although its water-wheels remained in operation until 1929. By this stage, Britain was no longer the workshop of the world and its industrial clout was hugely diminished. New Lanark's closure was announced in September 1967, and it was shuttered the following March before falling into dereliction. A local charity saved it from destruction and, now a UNESCO World Heritage Site, it stands as a monument to Britain's pivotal role in the Industrial Revolution.

UNIVERSITY OF GLASGOW

In 1712, Thomas Newcomen (1664–1729) invented a steam engine that effectively pumped water, and it was put to use in mines across Britain. It was fuel-inefficient and its movement was too imprecise to drive machinery. Watt, employed by the University of Glasgow repairing and making scientific instruments, truly harnessed steam's power. In 1763, he began improving a model Newcomen engine that the university owned. This was the foundation of the new engine that, in collaboration with his business partner Boulton, was introduced in 1775 and was instrumental in widening the applications of steam power, particularly in manufacturing.

ANGOSTURA

. . . .

Few figures have had a more decisive impact on a continent's history than Simón Bolívar (1783–1830) has wielded on South America's. He was the leader of the revolutionary war against the Spanish colonial government during the early nineteenth century. His ambitious plans for independence were laid out in Angostura, a city on the·banks of the Orinoco in north-eastern Venezuela.

By the early nineteenth century, Spanish imperial power was in decline. With Spain embroiled in the Napoleonic Wars, its authority over its overseas colonies fragmented, particularly in the Americas. Beginning in 1808, numerous local bodies called *juntas* declared independence and established autonomous self-government. There remained many loyalists to the Spanish Crown, and open fighting between them and pro-independence forces broke out in 1810. In Mexico and Central America, the struggle for independence lasted until 1821. The breakaway from European colonial control also occurred in Brazil. In 1822, Pedro I (1798–1834), the son of the Portuguese king, had declared Brazilian independence and after a brief war was declared emperor. His son and successor, Pedro II (1825–91), oversaw a mostly strong, stable and constitutional regime until he was overthrown in a military coup in 1889, which led to the overthrow of the monarchy and the establishment of republican government.

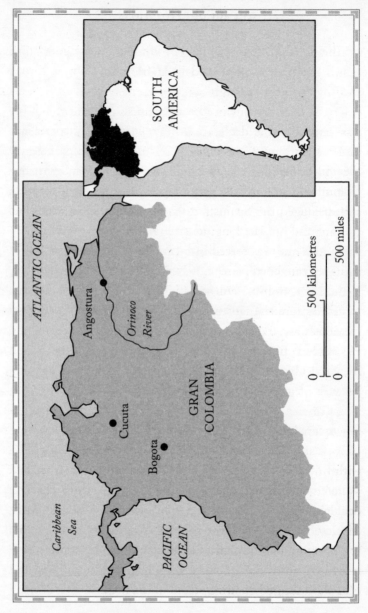

Gran Colombia, 1819–31

The process of national liberation took longest in Spanish South America. Bolívar had been born in Caracas into a wealthy aristocratic family, and spent many years in Europe, where he became convinced that Spanish rule must end. He was central to the declaration of Venezuelan independence in 1811 but could not prevent Spain retaking the country the following year. He fled to New Granada (modern-day Colombia), and in 1813 led an expedition to Venezuela and dislodged the Spanish, declaring himself president. His triumph did not last long; he struggled to gain the loyalty of the nation and was forced into exile in Jamaica in 1814 after being defeated by Spain.

In 1816, Bolívar returned to Venezuela, and in 1817 his forces captured Angostura, a city established five decades previously as a trading post between the coast and the interior. He made it his base to organize his new republic and plan the total liberation of Venezuela (the city also rose to fame because of a tonic that was developed from local tree bark by a Prussian surgeon in Bolívar's army that was marketed as Angostura bitters). The general who had overseen the capture of Angostura was Manuel Piar (1774–1817). He came to clash with Bolívar, and was consequently deprived of his command. When it became clear Piar might be a potential threat, Bolívar decided to make an example of him to establish his authority. In October 1817, Piar was called to Angostura to stand trial for insubordination, sedition, conspiracy and desertion. He was found guilty on all counts. Bolívar signed the warrant and Piar was executed by firing squad in the main square, flinging open his cape to reveal his chest and crying, '*Viva la Patria!*' as the bullets tore into him.

On 15 February 1819, Bolívar opened a congress in Angostura of twenty-six delegates who were fighting for the independence of Venezuela and New Granada. He made a speech laying out his vision for the future, stressing the importance of unity and centralization. That spring, Bolívar led a daring invasion of New Granada, advancing across plains, lakes and mountains to take the Spanish by surprise and defeat them at the Battle of Boyacá on 7 August. This secured independence for northern South America. Bolívar then returned to Angostura, where, thanks to his influence, on 17 December, the Congress declared the union of Venezuela and New Granada into the Republic of Colombia.

To differentiate it from the similarly named modern state it has become known as Gran Colombia. Bolívar, having completed the liberation of Venezuela, continued to campaign against the Spanish, expanding Gran Colombia to include modern-day Ecuador and Panama, as well as parts of Brazil, Guyana and Peru.

The debate over Gran Colombia's constitution was moved to the city of Cúcuta, where a congress met from 6 May to 14 October 1821. It created a centralized state, with its capital at Bogota and strong powers given to the president – an office that was duly taken up by Bolívar. Slavery was also abolished. Meanwhile, in the south of the continent, the struggle was spearheaded by José de San Martín (1778–1850), who led the United Provinces of the Rio de la Plata (which included much of modern-day Argentina, Bolivia and Uruguay) to

HAVANA HARBOUR

By the mid-nineteenth century, the only remaining Spanish possessions in the Americas were Puerto Rico and Cuba. In 1868–78 and 1879–80, Cuban rebels battled for independence, with war breaking out again in 1895. The conflict turned in January 1898 when the United States (where public opinion favoured the rebels) sent the armoured cruiser USS *Maine* to Havana Harbour to safeguard American citizens in the city. The next month it exploded and sank; the precise cause is still unknown. Regardless, it led to an American declaration of war on Spain, which surrendered that August. They handed over Puerto Rico (as well as Guam and the Philippines) to the United States, while Cuba gained independence.

independence in 1818. That same year, with San Martín's assistance, Chile became independent.

Despite being leader of the vast territory of Gran Colombia, Bolívar still sought to win independence for all South America. From 1824 to 1825, in concert with San Martín, Bolívar continued his activities, helping to achieve independence for Peru and Bolivia (the latter nation was named after him). While Bolívar was on campaign, Gran Colombia had grown more and more unstable. His return did little to ease the internal tensions that beset the nation. In April 1830, when it became clear that the republic he had helped to create was on the verge of breaking up, Bolívar resigned as president. He died of tuberculosis seven months later. Gran Colombia was dissolved within the year. In his honour, Angostura would be renamed Ciudad Bolívar in 1846; a great tribute, no doubt, but the man would have surely preferred the survival of a united and independent South America.

THE BLACK HILLS

. . . .

Set amid the plains between north-eastern Wyoming and western South Dakota are the forested slopes, peaks and valleys of the Black Hills. Sacred to several Native American groups, their story reveals the violence and perfidy they have frequently been subjected to.

By *c.* 28,000 BC, falling global temperatures had created a land bridge between Asia and the Americas that remained in existence until *c.* 14,000 BC. This allowed migration of hunter-gatherer groups from Asia who settled across the Americas. The indigenous peoples of North America established many diverse cultures; some adopted sedentary agriculture while others were nomadic, and the region was home to over fifty language families.

Europeans began to colonize North America in large numbers during the sixteenth century – their arrival was disastrous for the indigenous population. They brought with them diseases to which they had no resistance, and violence was all too common. As more and more European settlers arrived, the Native Americans found themselves forced off their ancestral lands. Many indigenous groups allied with European powers, often playing them off against each other. After the British won colonial dominance of North America in the mid-eighteenth century, it removed this option. Once the United States won independence in 1783, it pursued a long-term policy of westward expansion. In 1830, the Indian Removal Act gave the president the power to relocate Native Americans from their lands. As a result, in the south-eastern United States, around 100,000 Native Americans were forcibly removed and marched westward in brutal and inhumane conditions; around 15 per cent would die in this 'Trail of Tears'.

In 1848, the United States forced Mexico to cede its territories north of the Rio Grande; that year, gold was found in California. This ignited a gold rush that saw thousands of settlers move west, disrupting the hunting grounds in the territories they passed through. In an attempt to maintain peace, the United States government made a series of agreements with Native Americans, setting out their territory. For example, in 1868, the rights to the Black Hills were granted to the Sioux and Arapaho under the Second Treaty of Fort Laramie. However, within a few years this agreement would be brought into question.

George Armstrong Custer (1839–76) had fought for the Union during the American Civil War as a cavalry

CHACO CANYON

In the American Southwest, the indigenous population built structures of stone and adobe (a building material made of earth, water and organic materials like straw). These were often arranged as multistorey dwellings, with the entry to the rooms from below provided by ladders, which offered protection to the inhabitants. Spanish colonists called these settlements pueblos, from their word for town or village – many housed hundreds of people. One of their greatest concentrations is in Chaco Canyon, New Mexico, the home of several such complexes, and a major ceremonial and economic centre from around 850 to 1250, when it was abandoned due to drought.

officer, attracting attention for his bravery and flamboyant appearance (he favoured long blonde hair and sported a range of personalized uniforms), and winning promotion to brigadier general at the age of just twenty-three. When peacetime came, he was demoted because of the reduction in size of the army. He took part in several punitive expeditions against the Plains Indians of Kansas, and in 1868 oversaw the massacre of a Cheyenne encampment (including elderly, women and children) at the 'Battle' of Washita River. In 1874, Custer led an expedition to confirm reports that there were deposits of gold in the Black Hills. When he reported that there was indeed gold there, it sparked a great rush to the remote region. Despite the protections it guaranteed, the treaty was ignored as hundreds of gold hunters arrived.

The United States government wholly abrogated its previous promise, and in late 1875 ordered any Native Americans in the Black Hills region who had resisted the arrival of white prospectors to move to reservations by 31 January 1876 or face classification as 'hostile'. As it was winter, this request was unworkable. One of the leading figures who opposed the incursions into the Black Hills was Sitting Bull (*c.* 1831–90), a Lakota Sioux warrior who was part of the Hunkpapa group. Unified by his vision, that spring, hundreds of Sioux, Cheyenne and Arapaho left their reservations to join him at his encampment on the Little Bighorn River in southern Montana.

That May, three contingents of men from the United States Army marched west to meet Sitting Bull. Custer led the largest detachment, of about 700, which arrived at Sitting Bull's position on 25 June. When his men were spotted, Custer ordered an attack, splitting his command into three, thereby dangerously weakening them. He was unaware of the true strength of his enemy – he had been told there were only 800 warriors there, but in reality there were over 1,800. In the ensuing battle, Custer and his contingent of 210 men was isolated. They were all killed, as were fifty-five other American soldiers.

Ultimately. the military strength of the American government was too great for Sitting Bull. American reinforcements arrived, and in 1877 the Sioux and their allies were forced to give up their rights to the Black Hills and settle in reservations. Sitting Bull led his followers north to Canada, but the decline of the buffalo, which he and other Native Americans relied on for food (as well as using other parts of the animal to make a range of items including tipis, clothing, shoes and bowstrings), left them facing famine and they surrendered in 1881. Sitting Bull moved to the reservation at Standing Rock, but continued to resist the sale of tribal lands. After 1889, the Ghost Dance movement won adherents among the Sioux; it was inspired by a prophecy that a messianic figure would arrive to remove white settlers and oversee a return to the old ways. Fearing he could be a figurehead in a breakdown in order, the authorities ordered the arrest of Sitting Bull in December 1890; he was killed in a struggle when his allies tried to free him. By then, the vast majority of Native Americans had been forced to move to reservations, where to this day they have often faced harsh conditions, poverty and government attempts to forcibly 'integrate' them into Western culture.

KILMAINHAM GAOL

One of the great themes of the nineteenth and twentieth century was the struggle for national self-determination. In few places was this battle more contentious than in Ireland, with many of the key events playing out at the Kilmainham Gaol in Dublin.

English involvement in Ireland began in the twelfth century, when Anglo-Norman knights landed there. In 1171, Henry II (1133–89) invaded, and in 1177 he made his son John (1166–1216), who became king in 1199, 'Lord of Ireland'. Although the English Crown struggled to assert its control over the entire island, in 1542, Henry VIII (1491–1547) declared himself 'King of Ireland', a title subsequent English monarchs also claimed. During the sixteenth and seventeenth century, Protestant settlers from Scotland and England established plantations in Ireland, creating communities that eventually concentrated in the north. At this time there were frequent rebellions by Irish Catholics. However, by the eighteenth century, the British Crown dominated Ireland, although it retained its own parliament. In 1798, a revolutionary republican group called the United Irishmen launched a rebellion with French support. It was crushed within four months. Consequently, the Acts of Union came into law in 1801, joining Great Britain and Ireland into the United Kingdom.

Dublin, which had been founded by Viking settlers, had long been the centre of English power and influence in Ireland. During the eighteenth century, the city prospered, with considerable population growth and many new buildings. One of them was the 'New Gaol' in the suburb of Kilmainham, which replaced a run-down and unhygienic prison nearby. Opened in 1796, it was an imposing limestone and granite structure with two wings. However, its cells were cold and dark, and overcrowding and disease soon became a problem. As a result, from 1857 to 1861, the east wing was rebuilt. It had ninety-six well-lit cells and was inspired by the panopticon, a design where a single guard could theoretically observe any of the inmates.

Meanwhile, the course of Irish history had altered in 1845, when the potato blight arrived. This led to the failure of what had become the country's staple crop, causing four years of famine and disease, leading to 1 million deaths and 1 million emigrating. The Famine led to growing enmity against the British government in Ireland, with many believing the British had not been active enough in reacting to the crisis. In the years after the Famine, the Fenian Movement sprang up, its adherents willing to use violence to gain independence for Ireland. Many of their number, and other political prisoners, were held at Kilmainham. In contrast to the radical Fenians, there was a more peaceful campaign for 'home rule'. Its aim was to secure domestic self-government through legislation. After the failure of two home rule bills in 1886 and 1893, a third became law in 1914. It would have given Ireland its own devolved parliament, although the six most Protestant counties in Ulster would be temporarily excluded from the legislation. As a result of the First World War, the act was suspended. It would never be put into place.

By this time, Kilmainham Gaol was no longer operating as a prison; as an economy measure, it had been closed in 1910 and its inmates transferred elsewhere. The building was given to the British Army, who used it as a billet and military prison. In Easter 1916, with the British government occupied with the war, a group of Irish republicans staged a rising in Dublin. On Easter Monday, they seized several locations around the city, including the General Post Office. It was from the steps of that building that one of the rebellion's leaders, the writer, teacher and lawyer Patrick Pearse (1879–1916), read a proclamation declaring the independence of the Irish Republic. After six days of fighting with British forces, the rebels surrendered. Many of the leaders were captured and sentenced to death after a court-martial. Fourteen of them, including Pearse, were executed by firing squad in the yard at Kilmainham. One of them, the socialist James Connolly (1868–1916), had been wounded in the fighting; unable to stand, he was tied to a chair and shot. The men were not given the dignity of individual funerals or even a coffin – they were simply placed in a mass grave. The harsh response to the Rising led to a surge in support for republicanism, with the nationalist Sinn Féin party (which had been founded in 1905 and whose name meant 'we ourselves' in Irish) becoming increasingly popular. In 1918, Sinn Féin won seventy-three out of 105 Irish seats in Parliament, but refused to go to Westminster to take them up. Instead, in 1919, they established their own parliament in Dublin – the Dàil Éireann ('Assembly of Ireland').

Ireland was then plunged into war between republican and British forces, and Kilmainham resumed its role as a prison. The fighting was ended by the Anglo-Irish Treaty. This created the Irish Free State, a self-governing dominion. It partitioned Ireland, with six largely Protestant counties in the north-east being given the option to remain within the United Kingdom, which they duly did. The question of partition split Sinn Féin, and led to civil war between pro- and anti-Treaty groups breaking out in 1922. Kilmainham was controlled by pro-Treaty forces, and they used it to detain many of their former compatriots. The Irish Civil War ended in 1923, with the pro-Treaty side winning, and the last inmates left Kilmainham the year after. It was abandoned, and declared officially closed in 1929.

On 18 April 1949, the thirty-third anniversary of the Easter Rising, Ireland officially became a republic, wholly cutting any constitutional ties to the United Kingdom. Despite being the site of the martyrdom of heroes of the independence struggle, Kilmainham had become decrepit and overgrown with weeds. In 1958, a society with the aim of restoring it was founded. Thanks to donations and the work of volunteers, the site was restored and is now open to the public as a museum.

RED SQUARE AND THE KREMLIN

Russia's history is intrinsically bound up with Moscow; at the heart of the city is the fortified complex of the Kremlin and the neighbouring Red Square.

Moscow entered the historical record in 1147, when it was noted that Yury Dolgorukiy (c. 1099–1157), later Grand Prince of Kiev (and ruler of an area that included modern-day Ukraine, Belarus and western Russia), dined there. Nine years

later, a fortress was built in Moscow. Surrounded by a wooden wall atop earthen ramparts, it formed the basis of the Kremlin (possibly from the Greek for citadel), which would become the focal point of the small town that eventually grew into a city and a local principality. In 1237, the Mongols invaded Russia – when they arrived in Moscow the following year, the Kremlin could not stop them. Like many other towns, Moscow was captured, sacked and burned. The Mongols then established a polity called the Golden Horde, which enjoyed overlordship over Russia's many principalities, including Moscow. Despite being forced to pay tribute to the Mongols, the Princes of Moscow rebuilt their city and strengthened the Kremlin, as well as extending their power by absorbing other principalities. Eventually, the Princes of Moscow grew strong and large enough to lead the resistance to the Mongols during the fourteenth and fifteenth century.

THE WINTER PALACE

St Petersburg was founded by Peter the Great in 1703, becoming the Russian capital nine years later. In 1711, Peter had a Baroque residence, the Winter Palace, built for himself there. After a series of redesigns, it reached its final state in 1762. The finished Winter Palace had over 1,000 halls and rooms and symbolized Russian imperial power. After the February Revolution of 1917, the Winter Palace became the seat of the Russian Provisional Government, but under communist rule it was declared part of the Hermitage complex of art museums.

Ivan III – 'the Great' – (1440–1505) was the ruler who removed the Golden Horde's influence over Russia, defeating them in 1480. He extensively renovated and enlarged the Kremlin, employing builders and architects from Italy. The finished structure had over a mile (1.6 km) of brick walls and twenty towers. The Kremlin became both a royal residence and centre of government, as well as a major site for the Russian Orthodox Church. Three cathedrals were built around the Kremlin's central square. The oldest is the Cathedral of the Assumption, built between 1475 and 1479. The next is the Cathedral of the Annunciation, once the personal chapel of the Russia's rulers, first built in 1484–9 and reconstructed in 1562–4 after it burned down. Finally, there is the Cathedral of St Michael the Archangel, which was constructed in 1505–8 on the site of a fourteenth-century cathedral and was the burial site of the Russian tsars until the capital was moved to St Petersburg. Cathedral Square was used for important state occasions, and is still used during the inauguration of the President of Russia. At the same time as Ivan III remodelled the Kremlin, a new square was laid out directly to its east (it was originally separated by a moat that was later paved over). Red Square, as it became known, was around 74,322 square metres (800,000 square feet) in size and housed Moscow's largest market.

In 1547, Ivan III's grandson Ivan IV – 'the Terrible' – (1530–84) signalled Moscow's growing power by assuming a new title, 'Tsar of Russia', and extending its territory by campaigning against neighbouring states. To commemorate his military victories, he ordered the construction of the Cathedral of St Basil the Blessed at the southern end of Red Square. It was built in *c.* 1554–60 and its unique design and nine multicoloured towers have became a symbol of both Moscow and Russia itself. Despite periods of civil war and foreign invasion, the tsars continued to expand Russia's territory, particularly under Peter the Great (1672–1725). In 1712, he moved the capital to St Petersburg, and nine years later began to style himself as emperor. By the early nineteenth century, Russia was a great European power, but found itself drawn into the Napoleonic Wars. When Napoleon invaded Russia in 1812, he advanced as far as Moscow by September. As his army was approaching the city, a major fire broke out that destroyed two-thirds of its buildings. As a result, Napoleon took control of a desolate wasteland, and retreated after a month. During the rest of the century, Moscow was wholly rebuilt. The Kremlin was restored and a grand new palace built there. In 1872, the State Historical Museum was established at the northern end of Red Square. In 1893, a covered shopping complex with hundreds of shops, the Upper Trading Rows, was opened along the eastern side of the Square. It was nationalized under communist rule and renamed the Gosudarstvenny Universalny Magazin ('State Department Store' or GUM). It was closed in 1930 and used as government offices before being renovated and reopened as a shopping complex in 1953. Now privatized, GUM remains a popular shopping centre.

The Russian Empire was brought to a crashing end in 1917. With discontent widespread as a result of Russia's disastrous participation in the First World War, the February Revolution saw a mass uprising that led to the abdication of Nicholas II (1868–1918). The Provisional Government continued to fight the First World War, which remained highly unpopular. This allowed Vladimir Lenin (1870–1924) to lead his revolutionary party, the Bolsheviks, to power during the October Revolution. To solidify his power, he fought a long civil war against anti-communist forces that ended in

SMOLENSK

Smolensk, on the Dnieper River, is one of the oldest Russian cities, with a recorded history going back to the mid-ninth century. It was then an important point on the route between the Baltic and Black Sea, as well as that between Moscow and the rest of Europe. This location meant Smolensk was fiercely contested over the centuries. It was sacked by the Mongols, and also spent time under Lithuanian and Polish rule. Smolensk was burned by Napoleon's forces in 1812, and it was the site of savage fighting in 1941, during the Axis invasion of the Soviet Union.

victory in 1922, with the formal establishment of the Union of Soviet Socialist Republics. Lenin also moved the capital back to Moscow. The buildings of the Kremlin were used to house government offices. Red Square hosted numerous displays of Soviet strength and unity. The most high-profile were the military parades held on May Day and the anniversary of the October Revolution. After Lenin died, his embalmed body was put on display in a mausoleum on the west side of Red Square, where it remains on view to the public to this day.

The last great threat to Moscow's survival was posed by Nazi Germany. In June 1941, the Axis launched Operation

Barbarossa, their surprise invasion of Russia. By October, they were approaching Moscow, and much of its population was evacuated. Thanks to the fierce Soviet defence, the Axis forces were never able to reach Moscow and were forced to fall back. Although the city was seriously damaged in the fighting, it survived and the Kremlin and Red Square remained.

THE SOUTH POLE

. . . .

The southernmost point on Earth, the South Pole, is located in Antarctica, which remained entirely untouched by humankind until the 1820s. In subsequent decades, numerous expeditions attempted to reach the South Pole, with many ending in disaster.

The continent of Antarctica is around 14.2 million square km (5.5 million square miles) in size, and almost entirely covered by ice that has an average thickness of 2.4 km (1.5 miles). The waters that surround it are icy, treacherous and stormy, which means that for most of human history it remained isolated. Antarctica was first sighted in 1820, with Russian, British and American voyages all claiming the distinction. The first person to land on Antarctica may have been John Davis (b. 1784), an American who is believed to have briefly visited in 1821 in search of seals to hunt. However, for the most part the Antarctic remained undisturbed by humans until the 1890s, although several expeditions explored its coastline.

The British mounted an expedition to Antarctica in

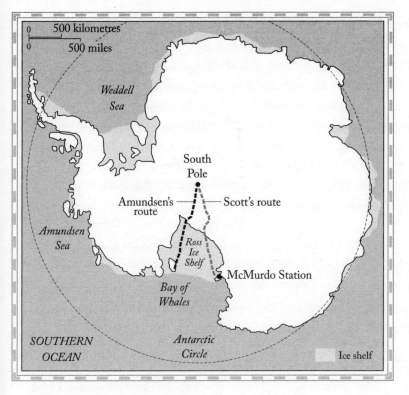

The race to the South Pole, 1911–12

1898, commanded by the Norwegian-born explorer Carsten Borchgrevink (1864–1934). Travelling in the *Southern Cross*, a steam-powered vessel built for sealing, they landed in Antarctica in February 1899. They established a camp, spending the winter there before exploring further south than anyone else had gone before, although they did not reach the Pole. Borchgrevink and his men returned safely in 1900, inspiring others to make similar voyages. They included the British *Discovery* Expedition of 1901–4, which explored further and conducted several scientific experiments (including launching an observation balloon). The expedition's party included two men who would become synonymous with the quest to be first to reach the South Pole: Robert Falcon Scott (1868–1912) and Ernest Shackleton (1874–1922). The latter man was the first to make an attempt – his *Nimrod* Expedition of 1907–9 came within around 160 km (100 miles) of the Pole but was forced to turn back.

In 1911, two parties attempted to reach the South Pole; one was led by Scott, while the other was a Norwegian team led by the explorer Roald Amundsen (1872–1928), who had already won fame by leading the first sea voyage through the Northwest Passage. Amundsen made use of sled dogs (most of which were later butchered to feed his men), and he and four others arrived at the South Pole on 14 December. He established a camp near there that he called Polheim, leaving a pitched tent and supplies behind. He and his men returned to their ship on 25 January, before sailing to Tasmania, where they were able to spread the news of their achievement around the world via telegram. Scott and his team of four men also reached the South Pole, although they only arrived there on 17 January 1912, thirty-four days after Amundsen. Scott and his men did not survive the voyage home; after failing to meet a resupply team from base camp, they all died. Their frozen bodies were discovered eight months later.

The next great ambition for explorers was to cross the Antarctic by land. In 1914, Shackleton returned to the continent

THE NORTHWEST PASSAGE

Before the completion of the Panama Canal in 1914, navigators searched for a sea route from the Atlantic to the Pacific that did not entail going around Cape Horn. One possibility was the Northwest Passage, a path through the Arctic Archipelago. Finding a safe passage through its islands and drifting icebergs was hazardous, and had eluded the efforts of many since the later fifteenth century. It was not until Amundsen's 1903–6 voyage that the Northwest Passage was found. Although originally thought impractical for commercial shipping due to ice coverage, recent global warming has made the journey easier to complete.

to do this, but before he could begin his attempt, his ship, the *Endurance*, became stuck in pack ice. After months of drifting, it was crushed and sunk in October 1915, leaving Shackleton and his men marooned. They then used lifeboats to travel to Elephant Island, which lay 240 km (150 miles) off the Antarctic. Shackleton then took five men to sail about 1,300 km (800 miles) across open sea to South Georgia, a British possession in the South Atlantic, in a modified lifeboat that was only 6.8 m (22.5 feet) long. In a spectacular feat of seamanship, he arrived there and arranged a rescue expedition to Elephant Island.

Miraculously, all of his men survived the ordeal. It would not be until the Commonwealth Trans-Antarctic Expedition of 1955–8 that the continent was traversed. Funded by a mixture of private donations and the British, New Zealand, American, Australian and South African governments, it was led by the English explorer Vivian Fuchs (1908–99), and also included the New Zealander Edmund Hillary (1919–2008), who had recently conquered Everest. Using tractors and supported by aeroplanes, they successfully traversed the Antarctic (via the South Pole) from 25 November 1957 to 2 March 1958.

MOUNT EVEREST

In 1852, Radhanath Sikdar (1813–70), an Indian mathematician, calculated that the Himalayan peak known as Chomolungma ('Goddess of the Valley' in Tibetan) was the tallest mountain in the world, with a height of 8,839 m (29,000 feet) – subsequent calculations showed his figure was only 10.6 metres (35 feet) below the actual elevation. It was subsequently renamed Everest after the British surveyor-general of India. After several attempts to climb Everest failed, it was conquered by a British expedition in 1953, with Hillary and the Nepali-Indian Tenzing Norgay (1914–86) being the first to reach the summit.

With interest in the Antarctic resuming and its precise status under international law unclear, in 1959, the twelve countries with interests there (Argentina, Australia, Belgium, Chile, France, Japan, New Zealand, Norway, South Africa, the Soviet Union, the United Kingdom and the United States) signed a treaty regarding the continent in Washington, D.C. on 1 December 1959. Amid the tensions of the Cold War, they agreed that the Antarctic should be a demilitarized zone with no military bases or weapons testing, with freedom to conduct scientific investigations that were encouraged to cooperate. Numerous research stations were established there, and in 1991 a new protocol set out the procedures to protect Antarctica's environment, with commercial attempts to find minerals or oil there banned until 2048. However, the main threat to Antarctica is climate change, which has led to rising water temperatures in the region and the rapid loss of ice.

THE MODERN WORLD

· · ❧ · ·

HOLLYWOOD

· · · · · · · · · · · · · · · · · · · ·

The twentieth century saw the global emergence of cinema, which became the world's most popular art form. The American film industry was central to this, and became synonymous with the Hollywood neighbourhood of Los Angeles.

During the later nineteenth century, inventors experimented with simple motion-picture technology. This developed into motion-picture films, which were short sequences shot by a single camera. The first public screening took place in Paris in 1895; it was held by the Lumière brothers Auguste (1862–1954) and Louis (1864–1948), who had invented a motion-picture camera called the cinematograph. Within a decade, movie theatres were operating in towns and cities across Europe, and huge crowds were paying to watch films that were becoming longer and increasingly sophisticated. As they were soundless, they were usually accompanied by live music played in the venue.

The United States was quick to adopt this new technology and art form, with its film industry initially concentrated on the East Coast. In 1893, the inventor Thomas Edison (1847–1931) opened a movie studio at his laboratories in West Orange, New Jersey. The first 'capital' of American cinema was Fort Lee, New Jersey, just outside New York. From 1907, film companies began building studios there, attracted by the cheaper and more abundant land. Studio bosses soon realized that a location with more reliably sunny weather (artificial lighting was in its infancy) and access to more varied locations would be preferable. They would alight on Hollywood, which was part of the Californian city of Los Angeles.

Prior to the arrival of the first Spanish explorers in 1542, California was home to several Native American peoples. European colonization began during the later eighteenth century, and was relatively small-scale. In 1781, the Spanish founded a small settlement in an area of desert they dubbed 'El Pueblo de la Reina de los Angeles' ('Town of the Queen of the Angels') – better known as Los Angeles. California became part of Mexico when it won independence from Spain in 1821, and in 1848 the United States gained control of it following the Mexican–American War. That year, gold was found there, leading to a rush of settlers. This population influx led to California winning statehood in 1850. Meanwhile, Los Angeles had become a city, which grew rapidly after it was connected to the national railway network and had its port enlarged and improved.

Hollywood began as a ranching and farming community, developing into a small town in the later nineteenth century

and formally merging with Los Angeles in 1910. That year, *In Old California*, the first film entirely shot in Hollywood, was produced, and in 1911 a movie studio was opened on Sunset Boulevard. Over the next decade, more and more studios would set up in Hollywood, often relocating from the East Coast, building huge filming lots and sound stages. This began a 'golden age' of American cinema lasting until the 1960s, which created styles, conventions, techniques and aesthetics still highly influential today. The period also saw the production of features with synchronized sound as well as in colour. In 1923, the famous 'Hollywood' sign (which originally read 'Hollywoodland' – the last four letters were removed during restoration work in 1949, and the entire sign was rebuilt in 1978) was built in the hills overlooking the area. That year, another long-term staple of cinema arrived in Hollywood: Walt Disney (1901–66). He had been an artist and had experimented with making films based on animated drawings. His eponymous studio made a series of films that defined animation as a genre, and in 1955 he also revolutionized the entertainment industry by opening his own theme park, Disneyland, in Anaheim, a city around 48 km (30 miles) south-east of Hollywood.

OAKWOOD GRANGE

Louis Le Prince (1841–90) was a French inventor who experimented with cinematography, secretly developing a camera that could shoot moving pictures. In 1888, he used it to film a silent two-second sequence of family members in the garden at Oakwood Grange, a house in Roundhay, a suburb of the northern English city of Leeds. The footage is the oldest surviving motion-picture film.

During the Golden Age of Hollywood, which lasted from the 1910s to the 1960s, the 'Big Five' studios (20th Century Fox, Metro-Goldwyn-Mayer, Paramount Pictures, RKO and Warner Bros.) dominated American cinema. They not only produced films but also distributed and exhibited them, as well as controlling directors and actors by tying them to long-term contracts. The films they made were popular not just in the United States, but with audiences across the world. After the Second World War, Hollywood began to change. In 1948, the Supreme Court decided that the monopolistic practice of movie studios owning cinema chains that exhibited only their films was illegal, leading to the decline of the Big Five's power. Furthermore, the Hays Code, a censorious set of moral guidelines that had restricted the content of American films since 1930, began to break down and was abandoned by the 1960s, allowing cinema to grow more experimental and risqué. At the same time, Hollywood was caught up in the wave of anti-communist paranoia that swept the United States after around 1947. As part of a government investigation into communism, several leading figures in Hollywood were summoned to testify at hearings in Washington. Ten of them refused to, and were fined and jailed. They, and hundreds of actors, directors, writers and other professionals were then effectively banned from being employed by any American movie studio as a result of suspected communist sympathies. This practice of 'blacklisting' lasted for over a decade.

Perhaps the greatest damage done to Hollywood's dominance of cinema came as a result of the rise of television. This undercut cinema, leading to declining audiences and profits, although Hollywood then became a major centre of the growing television industry. Over time, many movie studios began to abandon Hollywood, moving to different areas of Los Angeles or even outside it altogether. The only major studio still located there is Paramount Pictures, although 'Hollywood' still remains a shorthand for the film industry based in Los Angeles. Half of American films are still produced around Hollywood, and it is still the location of the Academy Awards (popularly known as the Oscars), the ceremony held since 1929, which, despite its controversies, remains a global byword for cinematic excellence.

OLYMPIA THEATRE IN BOMBAY

The first full-length film made in India was *Raja Harishchandra*, which was directed and produced by the pioneering Dadasaheb Phalke (1870–1944). Its premiere was held at the Olympia Theatre in Bombay (now Mumbai) on 21 April 1913, and it quickly became a huge success, laying the foundations of the highly popular Indian film industry, whose films are the most watched in the world. Its largest sector is based around Mumbai, known as 'Bollywood', which produces Hindi-language films.

AMRITSAR

. . . .

Amritsar is not only a major centre of Sikhism, but the site of one of the most brutal events in British colonial history, the Jallianwala Bagh massacre, which galvanized the Indian independence movement.

The Punjab region was the birthplace of Guru Nanak (1469–1539), the founder of Sikhism. He quickly gathered followers for his new religion. After he died, he was succeeded by nine more gurus who all contributed to the establishment of Sikhism.

When the tenth guru died in 1708, their holy scripture, the *Guru Granth Sahib*, became the final and eternal guru.

Amritsar was formally founded in 1577 by the fourth Guru, Ram Das (1534–81). He ordered the creation of a large sacred tank of water known as the Amrita Saras ('Pool of Nectar'), from which the town took its name. Ram Das's successor, Guru Arjan (1563–1606), built a gurdwara (Sikh place of worship) at the centre of the tank in 1589. Known as the Harmandir Sahib ('Abode of God'), it was reached by a marble bridge and was at a lower level than the rest of the town to remind worshippers of the need for humility. The Harmandir Sahib became the most sacred site of pilgrimage for Sikhs, and helped foster Amritsar's growth.

As Sikhism grew, its adherents often faced violent persecution, particularly at the hands of the Muslim Mughal emperors, who ruled Punjab and dominated the Indian subcontinent from the sixteenth to eighteenth centuries. As Mughal power declined during the eighteenth century, the Sikhs, who had formed armies to protect themselves, gained control of parts of Punjab, establishing several different states. In 1801, they were joined under the leadership of a military leader called Ranjit Singh (1780–1839), thereby founding the Sikh Empire. The next year, he paid for the Harmandir Sahib (which had been damaged several times since it was constructed) to be rebuilt in marble, copper and gold-leaf. It then became known as the Golden Temple. After Ranjit died in 1839, the Sikh Empire went into decline. This presented an opportunity to the East India Company, by then the ruler of much of the Indian subcontinent. After two wars, the Sikh Empire was dissolved in 1849 and placed under Company rule. When most of India rose up in rebellion against British rule in 1857, Punjab remained largely peaceful. The rebellion was defeated in 1858, after which the British government assumed direct rule of the Indian subcontinent.

PALASHI

By the mid-eighteenth century, the British East India Company had established itself in the Indian subcontinent, although it was by no means dominant. This changed in 1757, when the Company's forces defeated the rulers of Bengal, who were allied with the French, at the village of Palashi (anglicized as Plassey). This allowed the Company to install a puppet ruler of Bengal, laying the foundation for its establishment as the leading power in the Indian subcontinent.

By the early twentieth century, there was growing clamour for India to be given a greater degree of freedom. This escalated after World War I ended. British India had contributed heavily to the Allied war effort, with over 1 million serving overseas (Punjab had contributed more than any other province).

Many Indians hoped that this would persuade the British to allow greater self-government. Instead, on 21 March 1919, the legislature of British India passed the Anarchical and Revolutionary Crimes Act. This draconian measure extended emergency wartime measures against suspected political opponents. It allowed the colonial government to incarcerate and indefinitely detain people without due process, carry out trials with juries in secret, make arrests without warrant, and limit press freedom. Mahatma Gandhi (1869–1948), a former lawyer who was already an influential leader in the campaign for Indian independence, called for a one-day general strike to protest against the law. In Punjab there was widespread opposition to the law, although it remained peaceful until, when the leaders of the opposition were arrested, there was violence and rioting. On 10 April, police fired on a crowd of civilians in Amritsar, killing six and wounding more than thirty. Sir Michael O'Dwyer (1864–1940), Lieutenant Governor of Punjab since 1912, clamped down on this disorder by banning public gatherings. Reginald Dyer (1864–1927), who was in command of 1,185 troops in Amritsar (most of whom were Gurkhas or Baluchs), was tasked with preventing any further protests. On 13 April, Dyer heard that a large crowd (of about 10,000) had assembled at Jallianwalla Bagh, a walled garden near the Golden Temple. Dyer arrived at the gardens and had his men occupy the only exit. Without warning, he then ordered them to fire on the crowds. They killed 379 people (including a six-week-old baby) and wounded up to 2,000. Dyer then marched his men back to camp without helping any of the casualties lying in the gardens. Martial law was then extended over Punjab.

For his heartless actions, Dyer received a censure and was ordered to resign from the military, but no further punishment. When he returned to Britain in 1920, he was given a huge cash sum from money raised by sympathizers – he then went into retirement and died seven years later. O'Dwyer was relieved of his duties as Lieutenant Governor and also returned to Britain. In 1940, he was assassinated in Westminster by Udham Singh (1899–1940), a Punjabi Sikh and supporter of Indian independence, in retaliation for the Amritsar Massacre. Singh was arrested, found guilty of murder and executed by hanging.

News of the massacre spread across the Indian subcontinent. It persuaded the population that British rule was intolerable and must be campaigned against. Gandhi, in contrast to the violence of Amritsar, insisted on satyagraha (peaceful civil protest) against the British. Over time, support for the Indian independence movement increased. There was tension along religious lines, with some Muslims demanding that they should have their own separate state to guarantee their rights. After the Second World War ended, negotiations for Indian independence began. On 15 August 1947, India became independent, although Muslim-majority areas became their own separate state, Pakistan (whose eastern region, Bangladesh, split off in 1971). Partition led to the dislocation of millions, along with violence and rioting. Gandhi appealed for calm and held fasts but in 1948 was tragically assassinated by a

Hindu nationalist. Under the process of partition, Punjab was split in two, with the eastern part (which was mostly Hindu and Sikh) becoming Indian and the western, predominately Muslim, Pakistani.

Some Sikhs were dissatisfied with this state of affairs and began to demand their own separate homeland in Punjab. In 1984, Sikh separatists occupied the Golden Temple and surrounding buildings. When negotiations failed, Prime Minister Indira Gandhi (1917–84), no relation to Mahatma, ordered the army to remove them from the Golden Temple. They were attacked by Indian Army troops, and at least 450 people (including some unarmed pilgrims) were killed in the fighting. Five months later, Gandhi was assassinated by two Sikh bodyguards as an act of vengeance for the attack on the Golden Temple. Indira Gandhi's death led to mob violence against Sikhs across India. Fortunately, since the 1990s this kind of violence has been in decline and peace has largely returned to Punjab.

GLIWICE RADIO TOWER

. . . .

One of the main causes of the Second World War was Nazi Germany's invasion of Poland in 1939. To justify it, the Germans staged a deception operation in Gliwice; the prelude to the war that would be the most destructive conflict in human history, leading to the deaths of around 50 million people.

Gliwice is in Upper Silesia, the south-eastern part of a region mostly in Poland (with some parts in Germany and the Czech Republic) that has rich mineral resources, most importantly of coal and iron ore. The city, which received a charter in 1276, was originally under the control of the Silesian branch of the Polish Piast dynasty, before passing into the possession of Bohemia in 1335. After the Austrian Habsburgs inherited the Bohemian crown in 1526, they also gained Gliwice, which was also known by its German name, Gleiwitz. In 1742, Prussia conquered Silesia, which became part of the German Empire when it was created in 1871. Gliwice, like many towns in the region, industrialized during the nineteenth century, becoming an important centre of manufacturing, particularly of iron.

The First World War transformed Europe. Poland, which had been wiped from the map after a series of partitions divided it between Austria, Prussia and Russia, was recreated as an independent republic. Under the Treaty of Versailles, Germany experienced extensive territorial losses, including parts of Silesia that were granted to Czechoslovakia and Poland.

STALINGRAD

The Battle of Stalingrad was the most destructive battle in history, with around 2 million casualties. Stalingrad (now Volgograd) was an industrial and transport hub on the Volga River that was a major target of the Axis summer offensive in 1942. The struggle over the city lasted for over five months, with bitter house-to-house fighting, and culminated in the Red Army encircling their enemy and forcing their surrender in February 1943. The defeat was disastrous for the Nazis, and was the turning point of fighting on the Eastern Front.

Many ethnic Poles remained in German-ruled Upper Silesia, which included Gliwice, leading to a series of separatist insurrections from 1919 to 1921. To stop the violence, the League of Nations held referendums in Upper Silesia, where the population were asked if they wanted to be under German or Polish rule. Around 40 per cent voted to join Poland, while the remainder preferred to remain part of Germany. Accordingly, a portion of Upper Silesian territory was granted to Poland, although the greater part of it, including Gliwice, stayed German.

After the Nazis gained control of Germany in 1933, their main foreign policy aims were to reverse the hated Treaty of Versailles, reunite all German-speaking people under their rule

PEARL HARBOR

Hawaii, an archipelago in the North Pacific that had been an independent kingdom, was annexed by the United States in 1898. The US Navy realized Hawaii's strategic value and in 1908 established a base at Pearl Harbor on the island of Oahu. On 7 December 1941, Japan launched a surprise pre-emptive attack on the base, sinking and damaging several ships and killing hundreds. This led to the Americans entering the Second World War on the Allied side, which would be crucial to their eventual victory.

and gain *Lebensraum* ('living space') to the east. Poland, which had secured political and economic stability after its re-creation, would be caught in the crossfire. In March 1938, Germany annexed Austria despite the fact that this was prohibited by Versailles. Hitler's next target was the Sudetenland, a part of Czechoslovakia with a majority ethnic-German population. After he threatened war to secure it, a conference was held in Munich that September, where the British and French attempted to appease Hitler by allowing him to annexe Sudetenland. This was not enough to satiate him; in March 1939, he invaded the rest of Czechoslovakia, some of which was formally annexed to Germany. The rest became a protectorate, from which the German client state of the Slovak Republic was created (in addition, Hungary and Poland annexed some Czechoslovak territory). Hitler's actions showed France and the United Kingdom that he was not to be trusted. The next natural target of his ambitions was Poland. Accordingly, the British and French governments made guarantees to Poland that they would declare war on Germany if its independence was threatened.

On 23 August 1939, Germany and the Soviet Union made a neutrality agreement, the Molotov–Ribbentrop Pact (named after their respective foreign ministers). Given their ideological differences, this shocked the world. The Pact also contained secret clauses that carved up Poland, Romania, the Balkans and Finland into German and Soviet spheres of influence. With these assurances that the Soviets would not interfere, and the conviction that the British and French would not act, Hitler stepped up his preparations to invade Poland. As part of the plans, German forces posing as Poles staged a false-flag attack on their territory. The place of this operation was Gliwice Radio Tower. It had been built in 1934 and, at 118 m (387 feet) high, was the tallest wooden structure in Europe. On the night of 31 August, SS troops dressed in Polish Army uniforms staged a capture of the tower. They made a short broadcast in Polish and, to add realism to the 'attack', planted several dead bodies (most of whom were prisoners from Dachau concentration camp, although one was a captured local farmer). This incident was one of many that occurred that day up and down the German-Polish frontier. On 1 September, German (and Slovak) forces invaded Poland. The Poles fought fiercely but were overwhelmed by the Germans, helped by their greater number of tanks and aircraft. Two days after the invasion, France and the United Kingdom both declared war on Germany, but they could do little to help the beleaguered Polish forces. To make matters worse, on 17 September, the Soviets invaded from the east, and by 6 October the fighting was over. Poland was once more wiped from the map, divided between Germany, the Soviet Union and the Slovak Republic. Poland, particularly its Jewish population, suffered terribly during the war, with over 6 million civilian deaths. The Polish Underground battled against the occupying forces, while the military personnel who escaped Poland fought alongside the Allies with valour and distinction.

In June 1941, the Axis powers launched Operation Barbarossa, their invasion of the Soviet Union. Although at first successful, this brought the Soviets into the war on the Allied side and would eventually lead to the downfall of Nazi Germany. By 1945, with victory assured, the Allies began to discuss the structure of post-war Europe. Despite offering assurances that Poland would be guaranteed democratic elections, it became part of the sphere of influence of the Soviet Union, and they installed a friendly communist regime there. Gliwice became part of the reconstituted Poland, and its radio tower was used to transmit state radio until 1955, and then employed to jam signals from stations based in Western Europe. Democracy was not fully restored to Poland until 1989 when, following a nationwide wave of strikes and protests, free elections were held, marking the beginning of the end of communist rule there.

FLENSBURG

Hitler committed suicide on 30 April 1945. Under the terms of his will, Karl Dönitz (1891–1980), commander-in-chief of the German Navy, succeeded him as President of the Reich, Minister of War and Supreme Commander of the Armed Forces. With Berlin on the verge of falling, Dönitz formed his government in the northern German port of Flensburg. It was only capital of a (much-diminished) Third Reich for a few days – on 7 May, Dönitz ordered a surrender, although the Flensburg Government remained in place until 23 May, when its members were arrested.

ANNE FRANK'S HOUSE

Anti-Semitism has been a lamentably persistent feature of world history. It culminated in the Holocaust, when around 6 million Jews were systematically slaughtered. One of the most lasting human symbols of this genocidal campaign is Anne Frank (1929–45).

By the Middle Ages, Jewish people had settled across Europe. They faced persecution and discrimination, and were often forced to live in separate neighbourhoods known as ghettos (from the area of Venice where Jews were compelled to live). At times of crisis, Jewish people were scapegoated, and often made the focus of mob violence. Some countries, such as England in 1290 and Spain in 1492, expelled them altogether. It was not until the later eighteenth century that countries began to extend full citizenship rights to Jewish people. Despite this, the nineteenth century saw the rise of pseudoscientific notions that Jewish people were racially inferior, and many political parties used hatred of them to court popular sentiment. The greatest violence against the Jews occurred in the Russian Empire. After Emperor Alexander II (1818–81) was assassinated in 1881, a rumour spread that Jewish people were responsible. This led to a series of anti-Jewish pogroms (organized violent rioting), and the government passed laws that stated Jews must only live in urban areas and could not buy rural property. As a result, over 1 million Jews fled Russia. The dawning of the twentieth century saw anti-Semitism continue to develop. A forged text called *The Protocols of the Elders of Zion* popularized a theory that the Jewish people were involved in a vast global conspiracy for world domination, while they also became associated with Bolshevism in the aftermath of the Russian Revolution. Anti-Semitism would become most influential in one of the nations where the Jewish people had become most assimilated into the population: Germany.

Alongside his nationalist appeals for a restoration of German greatness, Hitler also played on this long-term hatred. He and the Nazis blamed the Jewish people for Germany's defeat in the First World War, and claimed their continued existence in the country was a blemish that had to be removed. After the Nazis took power in 1933, they passed a series of laws that robbed German Jews of many of their civil rights. The Nuremberg Laws of 1935 declared they could no longer be German citizens, and three years later the Nazis organized *Kristallnacht* ('Night of Broken Glass'), a nationwide campaign of violence and destruction aimed at Jewish homes, businesses and places of worship. In the face of such treatment, thousands of German Jews fled, although many countries refused to accept them in large numbers. They included Otto Frank (1889–1980), a Frankfurt-based businessman who had resettled in Amsterdam with his wife Edith (1900–45) and two daughters. He worked for a food-products distributor, and later started his own company.

WANNSEE VILLA

Set amid two lakes formed by the River Havel, Wannsee is one of Berlin's most beautiful suburbs, and a popular recreation spot. The wealthy often had residences there, including the pharmaceutical manufacturer Ernst Marlier (1875–1948), who built a luxury villa in Wannsee in 1914. By 1941, it had been sold to the SS, and on 20 January 1942 it hosted a conference of leading Nazis at which the details of the Final Solution were discussed.

The Frank family lived peacefully in Amsterdam until 1940, when Germany invaded and occupied the Netherlands. The next year, under new anti-Semitic laws, Anne was forced to leave her school and enrol in a Jewish one. For her thirteenth birthday, in 1942, she received a diary, so beginning an account of the rest of her short life. That year, the Nazi leadership had decided upon their 'Final Solution to the Jewish Question' at the Wannsee Conference. Whereas previously they had considered the idea of resettling them outside Europe, at Wannsee they decided that they would be exterminated. This was to be done by a mass deportation of Jewish people in occupied Europe to concentration and extermination camps, the largest of which were in occupied Poland. There, they faced disease, malnutrition and being used as slave labour, while millions were murdered in gas chambers and then incinerated. In addition, *Einsatzgruppen*, SS death squads, roved across occupied Europe, carrying out summary executions of millions of people. As well as Jewish people, the Nazis killed over 5 million other 'undesirables', including Soviet prisoners, non-Jewish Poles, Slavs, the disabled, Roma, political opponents, gay men and Jehovah's Witnesses.

On 5 July 1942, Anne's older sister, Margot (1926–45), received a deportation order, which prompted the Franks to go into hiding the next day. Together with four other Jewish people, they sheltered on the top floor of his business premises at 263 Prinsengracht, a large seventeenth-century house in central Amsterdam. They were supplied by their non-Jewish friends but conditions were cramped in the 'Secret Annex', a set of

PALACE OF JUSTICE, NUREMBERG

It was vital to hold the Nazis to public account for their methodical genocide against the Jews and other war crimes. An international tribunal was arranged – the location was Nuremberg, a Bavarian city that had hosted some of the largest Nazi rallies. Trials were held at the Palace of Justice, a complex of courts, offices and a prison. The first round ran from 20 November 1945 to 1 October 1946. Twenty-four leading Nazis were tried – half were sentenced to death. From 1946 to 1949, there was a series of twelve more trials at Nuremberg to prosecute other Nazis.

rooms accessed through a staircase hidden by a bookcase. Anne wrote in her diary every day until 1 August 1944. Three days later, the Gestapo discovered the hiding place, possibly having been tipped off by Dutch informers. Anne and her family were taken to a transit camp, and then sent east, arriving in Auschwitz in Poland on 3 September. From there, Anne and her sister Margot were transferred to the camp at Bergen-Belsen, where they both died in early 1945, probably of typhus. Their parents remained at Auschwitz, where Edith died of starvation, while Otto survived until the camp's liberation by the Red Army. After the war, he returned to Amsterdam, where friends who had searched the Secret Annex gave him his daughter's diary. After much consideration, he decided to publish it in Dutch in 1947. The book went on to be translated into seventy languages, and is one of the most widely read accounts of the Holocaust. In 1957, Otto helped found the Anne Frank Foundation, which saved the Prinsengracht house from planned demolition. The Foundation purchased the house, restored it and opened it as a museum in 1960. It stands as a reminder of the hideous and malign impact of racism and discrimination.

MOUNT WASHINGTON HOTEL

Many of the foundations of the structure of the contemporary global economy and the conventions of international trade were decided upon in Bretton Woods, New Hampshire, in 1944, at a meeting of the Allied powers held at the Mount Washington Hotel.

In 1920, after the First World War, the League of Nations was established to help guarantee the collective security of its member states and promote disarmament. These ambitious aims were undone by the fact that the United States never joined, and also because the League of Nations could do little to stem the aggressive expansionism of fascist powers that led to the outbreak of the Second World War in 1939.

While the Second World War was being fought, the Allies were already looking to the future, and making plans to create a body that would replace the largely ineffective League of Nations. In January 1942, the Allied powers signed the 'Declaration by United Nations', which declared their pledge to secure total victory over the Axis as part of a commitment to preserve human rights across the world. This agreement would be the foundation of the later establishment of the United Nations (UN). By 1944, the Allies were making plans for the post-war world, and trying to find a way to address the huge economic problems it would face, as well as to ease international trade in the future. To that end, a conference of 730 delegates from all forty-four Allied nations was held that July.

The venue for this United Nations Monetary and Financial Conference was the Mount Washington Hotel, a palatial structure built from 1900 to 1902 and set in a secluded location amid the rugged New Hampshire countryside. The Bretton Woods Conference sat from 1 to 22 July, and led to the founding of two major organizations whose members now include nearly every country on Earth. Firstly, it established the International Bank for Reconstruction and Development, which would lend money to states to rebuild, initially mostly concentrating on the war-torn nations of Europe. It would later become part of the World Bank, which still seeks to promote economic development and provide policy advice. In recent years, it has begun to focus on social reforms by encouraging things such as gender equality, improved access to education and environmental sustainability. Secondly, the other organization founded at the conference was the International Monetary Fund (IMF), which aimed to help facilitate trade and economic cooperation between nations.

Member states paid into a fund every year, from which they were allowed to borrow if they faced financial difficulties. It was hoped that this would mean that the system of international payments between countries would be stable, which in turn would encourage peace and prosperity. In addition, one of the IMF's aims was to ensure exchange rates remained stable; initially, they were fixed around the value of gold and the US dollar, and member states were supposed to ensure they did not deviate too widely from this. After staging the conference, the Mount Washington Hotel reopened to the paying public and remains in operation.

The year after Bretton Woods, another international conference was held in San Francisco (this one attended by fifty nations), which produced a final charter for the UN. Among many other things, it created a Security Council that would help ensure world peace and have to approve any changes to the Charter; it had five permanent members (China, France, the Soviet Union, the United Kingdom and the United States), each of which had the power of veto. In addition, an annual General Assembly of all member states was to be held as a forum for discussion, policy-making and setting the budget. The UN Charter was signed in San Francisco on 26 June, and the body was formally established on 24 October (with the League of Nations being officially disbanded the following year). It had fifty-one founding members, all of which had been represented at San Francisco, with the exception of Poland, which had been excluded because its post-war status had still not been decided upon then. Although the Cold War soured relations between East and West, the UN has proved remarkably robust and fairly successful in meeting its founding goals of promoting peace, global cooperation and human rights. The admission of South Sudan in 2011 means the UN now has 193 full members (as well as two non-member permanent observers, the Vatican City and Palestine), meaning it covers the greater part of the world.

METHODIST CENTRAL HALL

The first UN General Assembly, the annual gathering of its original fifty-one member states, was held from 10 January to 14 February 1946. The location was Methodist Central Hall in Westminster, London, which had been completed in 1911 and could seat over 2,000 people. Since 1952, the UN General Assembly has met at its permanent headquarters in New York City – although in 1988, the session was moved to Geneva to allow the Palestinian leader Yasser Arafat (1929–2004) to address it after the American government denied him a visa.

The Bretton Woods system was central to the post-war economic boom that lasted for a quarter of a century. However, in 1971, the United States announced that its dollar could no longer be redeemed for the same value of gold bullion. No longer tied to the gold standard, this meant that eventually the exchange value of the US dollar and other currencies would now 'float', subject to the ebbs and flows of the market. In the aftermath of this decision, the gold standard was internationally abandoned. This led at first to inflation but in the long term was largely beneficial to the economy. The most serious economic disruption the world has faced since Bretton Woods was the 2007–8 Global Financial Crisis, where falling property prices in the United States triggered an international recession. Although disaster and a complete breakdown of trade was averted, there have been calls to hold a second Bretton Woods, which might set out reforms that would prevent a similar global crisis from occurring in the future.

THE MARACANÃ

One of the great socio-cultural trends of the twentieth century was the emergence of mass consumption of sport. No events have attracted as consistently large audiences as the Olympic Games and the Football World Cup, and the Maracanã in Rio de Janeiro is synonymous with both.

Although competitive athletic events took place across the ancient world, those held in classical Greece are the most well known and influential. By the ninth century BC, games were regularly held to mark religious festivals. The most famous were at Olympia in the north-western Peloponnese, in an area of countryside close to a monumental statue of Zeus. The earliest recorded Olympic Games took place in 776 BC – the only athletic event was a 210-yard (192 m) foot race. Over subsequent games, which were held every four years, longer races were added, as well as other events such as wrestling, long jump, javelin, discus, boxing and chariot-racing. Entry was restricted to free male Greeks (who all participated nude) who travelled from across the Hellenic world for the chance to win the victor's wreath. The Olympics continued after the Romans won control of Greece in the mid-second century BC, but their importance declined. Ultimately, their close relationship with paganism was what led to them being abolished by the, now Christian, Roman imperial authorities in *c.* AD 400.

MUCH WENLOCK

Dr William Penny Brookes (1809–95), a surgeon and local magistrate, was eager to promote physical fitness among the working class of Wenlock, a group of settlements in the English county of Shropshire. The 'Wenlock Olympian Games' were first held in the town of Much Wenlock on 22 and 23 October 1850, and consisted of a series of athletic events and other sports. It became an annual event (held to this day), and was the major inspiration behind Coubertin's revival of the ancient Olympics.

By the later nineteenth century, the urbanization and mechanization caused by the Industrial Revolution led to concerns about the health of the people, particularly the working classes. Likewise, imperialistic rivalry and mass conscription made many states eager to promote physical fitness and exercise. As the notion of 'survival of the fittest' gained currency, schools and academies invested more time in exercise. These trends were key inspirations for the French educator Pierre de Coubertin (1863–1937), the prime mover behind the revival of the Ancient Olympics during the 1890s. Thanks in large part to Coubertin's efforts, the International Olympic Committee was established in 1894, and the first modern Olympics were held in Athens two years later.

One of the sports added at the second Summer Olympics, held in Paris in 1900, was football (entry was only open to men's teams – women's football did not make its Olympic debut until the 1996 Atlanta Games). The sport had its roots in games played in Britain since the medieval era, where neighbouring villages would compete en masse to drive a ball, by any means necessary, through some kind of goal (sometimes the entrance to the opposing team's parish church). By the nineteenth century these, often violent and chaotic, games had begun to be codified by different sporting clubs and schools. In 1863, the Football Association (FA) was established in London; a set of rules was agreed on, and clubs across England joined to compete with each other. Football then began to spread outside its birth-country; the Scottish Football Association was established in 1873, the year after England and Scotland had played the world's first-ever international football match. By the end of the century, organized football was played across the world, often spread by British workers or educators. In 1904, the International Federation of Association Football (better known as FIFA, from the initials of its French name) was founded in Paris to govern competition between nations. It now has 211 members – more even than the UN's 193.

In few places was football adopted more passionately than in Brazil. Organized football was first played there during the later nineteenth century between sporting clubs whose membership was mostly composed of white elites. Participation eventually broadened out to include the working classes and the non-white population, and the game was promoted by those who wished to create a sense of national unity. Brazilian football has become synonymous with creativity and excellence, but at first the country's national team found global success elusive. They were knocked out of the first two World Cups, held in Uruguay in 1930 and Italy in 1934, in the first round, and could only manage third in the 1938 World Cup in France. After two World Cups were cancelled as a result of the Second World War, the 1950 tournament would be held in Brazil. A new stadium was built in Rio de Janeiro. A two-tiered bowl, it was officially named after a local journalist called Mário Filho (1908–66), who had been central to promoting its construction, but was better known by the name of the neighbourhood it was located in, Maracanã. The tournament culminated on 16 July, with at least 199,854 people packed inside the Maracanã (the actual attendance was over 5,000 more when non-paying spectators are factored in) to watch Brazil play Uruguay. The hosts needed only a draw to win the tournament but Uruguay shocked the world to run out 2–1 victors and so win the World Cup. With many believing victory had been assured, the defeat was seen as a national tragedy in Brazil. However, the nation would recover from this setback to win the World Cup in 1958 – the first of its record five victories (although Brazil has never won the Women's World Cup, which has been held since 1991). Despite the trauma of its inauguration, the Maracanã would become one of the cathedrals of Brazilian football, regularly hosting crowds of over 150,000 for club and international matches. Over the years, it fell into disrepair, so after Brazil won the right to host the 2014 World Cup, it was extensively renovated, with a reduced (but all-seater) capacity of 78,838. Although it hosted the final, Brazil was not involved, its team having been eliminated in the semi-final.

The Maracanã played a central role in the 2016 Summer Olympics, which were held in sites across Rio de Janeiro. It hosted the opening and closing ceremonies, as well as some football matches, and an indoor arena was built on an adjacent site. The staging of the Games in Brazil was controversial there – the country was going through a time of economic hardship, and many believed the money spent could be better employed helping the poor. Furthermore, the national leadership was embroiled in controversy amid allegations of corruption. A few weeks before the Games opened, there were mass protests near the Maracanã, which culminated in violent clashes with the police. Since the Games, the Maracanã has fallen into disrepair; a lamentable state considering its huge importance in sporting and cultural history.

KOREAN DMZ

. . . .

Since 1953, the Korean Peninsula has been divided into separate states, each of which espouses markedly different ideologies. While South Korea is democratic, North Korea is one the last remaining bastions of communism in the world; dividing the two is the Demilitarized Zone (DMZ).

After the Second World War ended, one of the great questions was the fate of Korea, which had been ruled by the defeated Japanese Empire since 1910. In 1945, the Soviet Union and the United States divided their respective occupation zones along the 38th parallel. Although this was only meant to be a temporary expedient, growing distrust meant neither of the two Cold War superpowers could agree on a solution for reunifying Korea. In 1948, the communist Democratic People's Republic of Korea was founded in the north under the leadership of Kim Il-sung (1912–94), a former guerrilla leader. The state in the south was the Republic of Korea, where elections supervised by the United Nations were won by the pro-American Syngman Rhee (1875–1965). Both states claimed sovereignty over the entire peninsula, which, combined with their ideological differences, led to frequent border clashes.

ĐIỆN BIÊN PHỦ

On 2 September 1945, Hồ Chí Minh (1890–1969), who had led the resistance against the occupying Japanese, declared Vietnamese independence. This was not accepted by France, the former colonial rulers, and war broke out between them and pro-independence forces in 1946. As Hồ was a communist, the struggle became a proxy for Cold War rivalries. The final major engagement was the French defeat at Điện Biên Phủ in north-western Vietnam in 1954. It led to their withdrawal and the split of Vietnam into a communist state in the north and a pro-Western one in the south. Conflict between them began in 1955; despite the United States intervening on South Vietnam's behalf, North Vietnam triumphed in 1975, reuniting the nation under its rule.

On 25 June 1950, having gained Soviet support for their actions, the North Koreans launched a mass invasion across the 38th parallel. Three days later they had captured Seoul, but the loss of their capital did not result in an immediate South Korean surrender. The American government, fearing that communist dominance of all Korea would lead to a domino effect whereby surrounding countries in the region would also follow, pledged to intervene. After gaining the support of the United Nations (UN), American forces began to arrive. Alongside combat personnel from fifteen other countries, they would form 90 per cent of the United Nations Command, the multinational force that supported South Korea. At first alongside their South Korean allies, the Americans fell back behind a defensive line called the Pusan Perimeter in the south-eastern corner of the peninsula, fighting desperately for survival until further reinforcements could arrive. They did that September, when UN forces counter-attacked by launching an amphibious invasion of the port city of Incheon, which led to the recapture of Seoul. This was followed by a UN advance across the 38th parallel, and a rapid drive north. China now formally intervened in the war, which led to the UN retreating south, below the 38th parallel, by the end of the year. At this time, although it was not officially involved in the conflict, the Soviet Union sent aeroplanes and pilots (who posed as Chinese or Korean) to join the struggle for aerial supremacy.

As the new year dawned, the main theatre of the increasingly attritional war was along the 38th parallel. Although the communists had a numerical advantage, the Americans were engaged in a devastating bombing campaign of North Korea. With casualties mounting and a clear path to victory for either side unclear, a negotiated end to the fighting became more and more attractive to all involved. Formal peace talks began in July 1951 at Kaesong, a city that had been the Korean capital from the tenth to fourteenth century. That October, they moved to the small village of Panmunjom. Even while negotiations were going on, the fighting continued, but neither side was able to make any significant gains. On 27 July 1953, the Korean Armistice Agreement was finally signed at Panmunjom. Although it was not a formal peace treaty, it declared that armed hostilities would end. Around the demarcation line between the two Koreas, which ran near the 38th parallel, a buffer zone 4 km (2.5 miles) wide, known as the DMZ, was established. Furthermore, there was an exchange of the thousands of prisoners of war held by both sides. Soldiers from the UNC, mostly American, remained in place to help guarantee South Korean security. In total, the Korean War had cost as many as 5 million lives, around half of whom were civilians.

The Korean DMZ remained fortified, and it is the most heavily armed border in the world, as well as the site of occasional skirmishes. The only place where troops stood face-to-face is the Joint Security Area, a complex of buildings near Panmunjom that was established as a neutral area for diplomatic meetings and negotiations. Life on either side of the DMZ is spectacularly different. North Korea continued to be a single-party totalitarian dictatorship under Kim Il-sung and his successors – first his son Kim Jong-il (1941–2011) and then his grandson Kim Jong-un (b. 1983). In addition to harsh political repression, the country experienced mass famine in the wake of the collapse of the Soviet Union, which had been a major supporter. Despite this, it has continued to invest heavily in its military capability, even developing nuclear weapons. South Korea's post-war history has been different. In the aftermath of the war it had been one of the poorest countries in the world but, from the 1960s on, experienced rapid economic growth. Furthermore, after a series of unelected military-backed rulers, the first democratic elections were held in South Korea in 1987. By then, the country had developed into a major centre of industry, and it is now one of the most developed and prosperous places on Earth.

SUKHOY NOS

Overshadowing the Cold War was the threat of nuclear annihilation. After the Soviet Union developed its own nuclear weapon in 1949, both they and the Americans carried out tests of increasingly powerful devices. The largest was the Tsar Bomba, which the Soviets detonated on 30 October 1961 at Sukhoy Nos, a testing site on Severny Island in the Russian Arctic. It created a mushroom cloud 64 km (40 miles) high and shattered windows as far away as Norway.

BAIKONUR COSMODROME

Cold War rivalries between the United States and the Soviet Union were not just played out on Earth, but in the heavens. Throughout the 1950s and 1960s, both superpowers vied with each other for dominance in the Space Race, with the Soviets building their main facility on the Kazakh Steppe.

After the Second World War, the Americans and the Soviets both developed increasingly sophisticated ballistic missile technology. To that end, each of them actively recruited German scientists and engineers who had worked in the Nazi missile programme. This was both a military and national security matter (the missiles were projected to be used to fire nuclear weapons), as well as a symbol of the ideological struggle between communism and capitalism. By the mid-1950s, the missiles were large and powerful enough to break Earth's orbit and send objects into space, the next theatre for Cold War competition.

One key feature of the Soviet missile and space programme was secrecy. In 1955, when they were building a new launch site for ballistic missiles, they needed somewhere that was relatively remote, in an area of open plains (so radio signals would not be interfered with) and as close as possible to the equator (where the Earth's surface rotated more quickly). The selected site was near a village called Tyuratam in an area of arid desert in southern Kazakhstan. To confuse foreign powers about its location they would later code-name the site Baikonur, which was also the name of a mining town over 320 km (200 miles) away.

With the launch site chosen, the Soviet governmental apparatus swung into action; railways and roads were built to connect Baikonur to the rest of the nation, and a town to house its workers sprung up around Tyuratam (in 1966, it would be given city status, and have its name changed to Leninsk, although it would also be known as 'Star City'). Although the site has become synonymous with space flight, it has also always been a proving ground for long-range missiles. In 1957, the Soviets successfully launched the R-7 Semyorka from Baikonur. It was the first-ever intercontinental ballistic missile, with a range of around 6,000 km (3,700 miles); later designs could travel even greater distances with a higher degree of precision. The missile was also powerful enough to be used to launch items into orbit.

KENNEDY SPACE CENTER

In 1962, seeking a site large enough to launch a rocket that could reach the Moon, NASA purchased land on Merritt Island, Florida, with construction beginning that year. It was adjacent to Cape Canaveral, the launch site for many previous NASA mission. The Kennedy Space Center was given its current name in 1963, after the assassination of the president whose challenge to send a man to the Moon had inspired its construction. The Kennedy Space Center hosted the launch of Apollo 11, which made the first Moon landing on 20 July 1969, as well as several other lunar missions. Skylab, the first American space station, was also launched from there, and it was also used for take-off and landing of space shuttles.

At first the Soviets dominated the Space Race, with Baikonur Cosmodrome hosting a series of successful launches. On 4 October 1957, an R-7 rocket was used to launch Sputnik 1 from Baikonur. Weighing just 83.6 kg (184 pounds), this was the first man-made satellite to orbit Earth, completing a circuit every ninety-six minutes until it fell back into the atmosphere and burned up the following year. Just one month after the first launch, the Soviets launched Sputnik 2, which carried a stray dog called Laika – she was the first living creature to go into space. She died around six hours into her mission, from a combination of shock and overheating. The culmination of this era of Soviet success was the launch of Vostok 1 (a variant of the R-7), which carried a capsule containing Yuri Gagarin (1934–68), a former air force pilot, into outer space. During his 108-minute long mission, he became the first human to achieve orbital flight. The mission was a huge propaganda coup for the Soviet Union.

Gagarin became a worldwide celebrity but was not given any more space missions, as the Soviet authorities did not want to risk the death of such a high-profile figure. Despite this precaution, he would die prematurely in 1968, in a plane crash during a training flight. The first woman in space, Valentina Tereshkova (b. 1937), a former textile worker and amateur skydiver, also left from Baikonur in 1963.

Soviet dominance of manned spaceflight ended during the mid-1960s. In response to President John F. Kennedy's (1917–63) challenge to land a man on the Moon by the end of the decade, the American National Aeronautics and Space

Administration (NASA) redoubled its efforts (helped by a 500 per cent budget increase) and eventually overtook the Soviets. The Americans would make the first of six successful landings on the Moon in 1969. Meanwhile, between 1969 and 1972, the four Soviet attempts to launch a lunar mission all failed, although they did achieve a major success in 1971, when they launched Salyut 1, the first-ever space station, from Baikonur. The Space Race effectively ended in 1975, with the joint Soyuz–Apollo mission, where an American and Soviet craft docked together in orbit, and the crews carried out scientific experiments.

In 1991, the Soviet Union broke up, and the Kazakh Soviet Socialist Republic became the independent nation of Kazakhstan. However, the Russians made a deal with the Kazakh government to be allowed to continue to use Baikonur Cosmodrome for their space programme in exchange for an annual rent of $115 million. Four years later, symbolic of the rolling-back of communism, the city of Leninsk's name was officially changed to Baikonur. It remains a great hub of space flight and exploration, used for space shuttles and unmanned spacecraft. Its greatest role today is as one of the most important departure points for missions to the International Space Station, an orbital facility that hosts scientists, astronauts, cosmonauts and space tourists from across the world (with visitors from eighteen different countries so far), which has been in continuous operation since its launch in 1998.

SHARPEVILLE POLICE STATION

Under apartheid the non-white population of South Africa was often relocated to racially segregated areas called townships. Conditions there were mediocre, with poor infrastructure and limited employment. The most infamous township is Sharpeville, the location of an atrocity that transformed South African history.

During the 1950s, 1960s and 1970s, countries across Africa won their independence as European powers divested themselves of their colonial possessions in the aftermath of the Second World War. The situation in South Africa was different. Following the Second Boer War (1899–1902), the Union of South Africa had been created in 1910 by joining two British

WITWATERSRAND

South African history was transformed by a ridge of rock called Witwatersrand. In 1886, it was discovered that it had rich gold deposits, sparking a rush of migrants. Witwatersrand was part of Transvaal, one of two independent republics (the other is Orange Free State) established by the Boers, Afrikaans-speaking descendants of European, mostly Dutch, settlers. Control of Witwatersrand was one of the central causes of the Second Boer War, which began in 1899. After a bitter struggle the British won victory in 1902, having deliberately targeted the civilian population to force the Boer republics to surrender.

colonies and two Boer Republics. Since its inception it had enjoyed domestic self-government, and in 1931 the Statute of Westminster had effectively given the nation independence by removing the British Parliament's right to legislate for it. The minority white population dominated South Africa's political and economic life through the systematic disenfranchisement of black voters and laws that limited their rights to hold property. There was also informal social segregation on racial lines. After 1948 this was formalized through the system of apartheid ('separateness' in Afrikaans), a series of laws that enforced white supremacy. All South Africans were registered by race, which determined where they could live and work, and there was strict segregation of public facilities.

These racist policies prompted a backlash against the South African government abroad, with many states condemning its actions and enacting trade embargoes. Domestically, by the 1950s, a widespread anti-apartheid movement had coalesced, which saw mass protests and demonstrations across the country. The government reacted by clamping down on any resistance, attempting to silence any dissenting voices through violence, censorship and arrests. The most important anti-apartheid organization was the African National Congress (ANC), which had been founded in 1912 to fight for equal voting rights. One of its leading members was Nelson Mandela (1918–2013), the son of a clan chief. He, and many ANC members, originally mostly favoured non-violent methods and passive resistance in their protests, but their opinions changed as a result of what occurred in Sharpeville.

One of the foundations of apartheid was the separation of the country into separate zones for different racial groups. These were enforced by the pass laws, which made all black people aged over sixteen carry identification documents if they travelled outside restricted areas. Those who did not have valid documentation faced arrest. These pass books were much hated, and were often burned by protesters as a symbol of resistance to apartheid. In 1960, the Pan-Africanist Congress, a group that had broken away from the ANC the previous year, announced a national demonstration against the pass laws. It would take place on 21 March (ten days before the ANC planned to launch their own anti-pass protests).

That day, there were protests across South Africa. The PAC called on people to stop carrying their passes and demand to be arrested, hoping their actions would bring the nation to a standstill. That morning at Sharpeville, crowds gathered around the police station, reaching over 5,000. The demonstrations were mostly peaceful, with the crowds singing songs and chanting slogans. The police responded by ordering aircraft to fly low over the crowds, while reinforcements in armoured cars were sent in, raising police numbers to 300. At around 1.15 p.m., there was a surge in the crowds. Without warning, one policeman fired, then many of his colleagues followed suit. After two minutes, sixty-nine protesters had been killed and around 200 wounded. Many of them had been shot in the back as they tried to flee. After the massacre, riots, marches and strikes swept the nation. The government declared a state of emergency, and banned the ANC.

In the aftermath of Sharpeville, the United Nations called on the South African government to end apartheid. Mandela realized that more militant methods would be needed to achieve this. He then helped to found Umkhonto we Sizwe ('Spear of the Nation'), the armed wing of the ANC, in 1961, which attacked government facilities and sabotaged infrastructure. Mandela became a wanted man and was forced to go underground. However, in 1962, after spending some time in Algeria being trained in guerrilla warfare, he was stopped at a roadblock and arrested before being sentenced to five years in prison for his actions. Mandela's situation worsened the following year, when, after a raid on an ANC hideout in the Johannesburg suburb of Rivonia, the police located plans for armed resistance, along with a cache of weapons. This led to Mandela and ten others being tried for conspiracy, sabotage and treason. At the ensuing trial, which concluded in 1964, eight of them (including Mandela) were sentenced to life imprisonment.

While Mandela languished in prison, the struggle against apartheid intensified. International sanctions meant that South Africa became a pariah state, and clashes between protesters and police became more common. With violence escalating, during the 1980s, secret negotiations began between the government and the ANC about how to end apartheid. This led to Mandela's release from prison in 1990 and the legalization of the ANC. After further talks, in 1994, elections were held where all South Africans could vote on an equal basis. The ANC emerged victorious and Mandela was charged with forming South Africa's post-apartheid government, serving as president until 1999. During his single term, he established a Truth and Reconciliation Commission to uncover the human rights crimes of the apartheid era, and in 1996 he promulgated a new constitution that permanently enshrined the equality of all South Africans under the law. The place he chose to sign it into law was Sharpeville.

CERN

· · · · · · · · · ·

More than any other recent innovation, the World Wide Web (WWW) has transformed society, politics and the world's economy by allowing huge volumes of information to be exchanged near-instantaneously. It started life at the European Organization for Nuclear Research (better known by the abbreviation of its original French name, *Conseil européen pour la recherche nucléaire*, CERN) – one of many cutting-edge innovations to take place there.

The European Council for Nuclear Research was provisionally formed in 1952 in Paris, with twelve founding member states contributing to its budget and operation (ten other countries have joined CERN – it now has twenty-two members and in 2014 welcomed Israel, the first non-European state to join). It was to be dedicated primarily to particle physics, the study of the smallest objects in existence, and to harness the collective power of scientists from different nations working together. CERN was officially established in 1954, when its constitution was ratified. At the same time the 'council' in its name was replaced by 'organization', but it continued to be known as CERN. According to its constitution, its research must be purely scientific and should not be focused on military requirements. Its work was not to be carried out secretively, but be made available to the public.

BOELTER HALL ROOM 3420, UNIVERSITY OF CALIFORNIA, LOS ANGELES (UCLA)

ARPANET was an important precursor to the internet. When it was launched in 1969 it had four nodes. One was at UCLA, in a small basement room, where on 29 October the first message was sent through ARPANET, to the Stanford Research Institute. It was 'lo' – the operator had been trying to type 'login' but the system had crashed before he could finish.

CERN's main site is in Meyrin, a small village (now a commuter suburb) outside Geneva, close to the French border. It eventually extended across the frontier, and now over 80 per cent of the facility is in France. The first great achievement at CERN was the construction of a particle accelerator in 1957. These devices are used to accelerate a beam of particles (such as electrons or protons) to high speeds in a vacuum and steer their progress using magnetic fields. Once the particles have reached their desired speed, they are made to collide with a target or another beam, with detectors recording the outcome of the event. This enables scientists to find out more about the nature of the fundamental building blocks of the universe, and observe the behaviour of the particles. Over the decades, many more particle accelerators were built at CERN. They include the Large Hadron Collider (LHC), an underground ring, 27 km (17 miles) in length, that passes into French territory. Built from 1998 to 2008, it went into full operation in 2009. Experiments in the LHC confirmed the existence of a hitherto only theorized Higgs boson, which gives all particles mass.

The internet is simply a network that allows computers to connect and share information with each other. One of its earliest iterations was the Advanced Research Projects Agency Network (ARPANET), which was established in 1969 and funded by the United States Department of Defense. It used a method called packet switching, which broke up data into small pieces and reassembled them at their destination, which allowed far quicker transmission. During the 1970s and 1980s, the internet was little known outside a small circle of academics, scientists and public officials. This would all change thanks to work done at CERN.

PALAZZO DEI CONSERVATORI

CERN was not the only pan-European organization established after the Second World War. The most politically significant was the European Union, which originated as the European Economic Community. It was created by the Treaty of Rome, signed by the six founding members (Belgium, France, Italy, Luxembourg, the Netherlands and West Germany). The ceremony took place at the Palazzo dei Conservatori, a medieval palace that had been renovated by Michelangelo during the 1530s.

In 1989, a British engineer and computer scientist working at CERN, Tim Berners-Lee (b. 1955), was working on a system for scientists from different countries to easily transfer electronic files between computers using the internet. He proposed the WWW as a solution to this problem. He then developed the first-ever website, which went live on 6 August 1991 and contained information about how to use and develop the WWW. Berners-Lee, in line with CERN policy, then made the WWW's software freely available for the public to use in 1993. This, along with the falling price of personal computers (which were also becoming more powerful than ever), led to the explosion of the internet and its emergence in the public sphere. From 1990 to 2000, the number of internet users worldwide grew at a spectacular rate – from 2.6 million to over 400 million. There are now well over 3 billion internet users, representing nearly half of the population of the world. Many will access it using mobile devices, which have allowed people to maintain near-constant connectivity to the WWW.

The ubiquity of the internet, particularly in the developed world, is a fundamental feature of twenty-first-century society. Tech companies wield huge power over our daily lives, with the 'Big Five' (Amazon, Apple, Facebook, Google and Microsoft) dominating the sector. The WWW and internet have not always lived up to the idealism fostered at CERN. In many ways, although supposed to bring people together, the technologies may have encouraged a sense of alienation from society among some, and have also raised fears about the risks of digital surveillance of our online, and even our domestic, activities and rampant commercialization of our personal data. Having said that, the internet and WWW have positively impacted humanity in many ways, including providing instant communication, enabling the sharing and preservation of digitized data, and helping to streamline economic transactions. Regardless, it is clear that Berners-Lee's idea at CERN has, and continues to, transform the world.

CONCLUSION

Every corner of the world has the potential to be the site of history. Even long-term trends can often be crystallized to a single location, for example, the story of the creation of the industrialized global economy can be told through an inn in Bruges, a small Scottish village and a commuter suburb of Geneva. The rise of ancient civilizations in Egypt and China can be uncovered through the Yellow River and the Nile. Epochal figures are often inextricably tied to a place that illuminates their stories – how can one tell the story of figures like the Buddha or Louis XIV without understanding the Bodhi Tree or the Palace of Versailles? The great conflicts that have shaped our history can often be traced back to a single location, such as a radio tower on the German–Polish border.

As we move towards spending more time in the digital environment, there may be a few that doubt epochal moments in history can always be tied to a physical place. However, the internet does exist in a tangible sense in places such as server farms and data centres, which may well be the locations that shape tomorrow's history. Finally, even if humanity colonizes the stars, there is no doubt that the scientific breakthroughs and political decisions that made this happen will have a root somewhere in the world.

Acknowledgements

This book would not have been possible without the brilliant team at Michael O'Mara Books, particularly my editor Gabriella Nemeth. I would also like to thank David Inglesfield for his copy-editing work, Aubrey Smith for the illustrations and David Woodroffe for the maps. Thank you also to my students and colleagues for their insights and discussions over the years. Finally, my sincerest gratitude to the amazing people at the British Library for the incredible work they do.

Select Bibliography

Field, J.F., *The History of Europe in Bite-sized Chunks*, Michael O'Mara Books, 2019

Finkel, C., *Osman's Dream: The Story of the Ottoman Empire 1300-1923*, John Murray, 2006

Grant, R.G. (ed.), *1001 Battles That Changed the Course of History*, Cassell, 2011

Grine, F.E., Fleagle, J.G., and Leakey, R.E. (eds.), *The First Humans – Origin and Early Evolution of the Genus Homo*, Springer, 2009

Judt, T., *Postwar: A History of Europe Since 1945*, Vintage, 2010

Loewe, M. and Shaughnessy, E.L. (eds.), *The Cambridge History of Ancient China: From the Origins of Civilisation to 221 BC*, Cambridge University Press, 1999

Mango, C. (ed.), *The Oxford History of Byzantium*, Oxford University Press, 2002

Oliver, R. and Atmore, A., *Medieval Africa, 1250-1800*, Cambridge University Press, 2001

Seth, M.J., *A Concise History of Korea From Antiquity to the Present*, Rowman & Littlefield, 2016

Shaw, I. (ed.), *The Oxford History of Ancient Egypt*, Oxford University Press, 2000

Speake, G. (ed.), *Encyclopedia of Greece and the Hellenic Tradition*, Fitzroy Dearborn, 2000

Van De Mieroop, M., *A History of the Ancient Near East ca. 3000-323 BC*, Blackwell, 2004

INDEX